THE POWER

THE POWER OF YOU

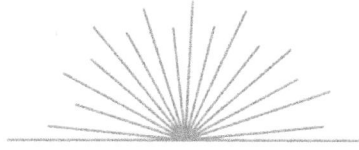

THE

POWER

OF

YOU

Unlock Your Inner Potential and

Manifest the Life of your Dreams.

Written By

Lisa Renée Ruggeri

www.lisareneeruggeri.com

THE POWER OF YOU

Disclaimer:

The information presented in The Power in You is intended for educational and informational purposes only. The concepts and techniques discussed are based on the principles of Neville Goddard's Law of Assumption, quantum physics, CBT and personal development. While these ideas can be empowering and transformative, they are not a substitute for professional medical or psychological advice.

The content of this book is based on the author's interpretation of these principles and their application to personal development. Individual results may vary, and the effectiveness of the techniques described is not guaranteed. The author and publisher do not claim that these practices will cure or prevent any medical or psychological conditions.

If you have any health concerns, including physical, mental, or emotional health issues, please seek the advice of a qualified healthcare professional. This book is not intended to diagnose, treat, or provide medical or psychological advice. Always consult with a licensed professional before making any significant changes to your health or well-being.

By reading this book, you acknowledge that the author and publisher are not liable for any adverse effects or consequences resulting from the use or application of the information provided. Your use of this book's content is at your own discretion.

Dedicated to:

The ones who have shined a light on my journey—
Your guidance, love, and unwavering support have illuminated
my path in ways words can barely capture.
This book is for you, the beacons in my life who've made every
step brighter.

Thank you for walking this journey with me.

Contents

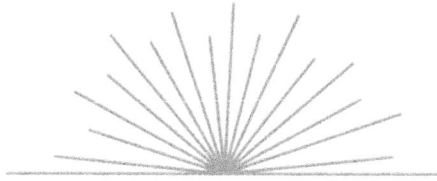

Chapter 1

Unlocking the Magic Within

Imagine waking up one morning and realizing that everything you've ever dreamed of is within your grasp. The life you've always wanted—the success, the love, the happiness, the freedom—isn't just some distant fantasy. It's a reality that you can create, starting right now. This isn't a fairy tale. It's the power of manifesting your dream life, and it's all rooted in one simple yet profound truth: your thoughts create your reality.

At first, this might sound like a lofty promise or a too-good-to-be-true pitch. But consider this: every great accomplishment, every breakthrough, every significant change in history began with a single thought. The people who have achieved extraordinary things weren't necessarily the smartest, the richest, or the luckiest. What set them apart was their belief in something greater, their unyielding conviction that they could shape their destiny. They tapped into the magic within them, and they made the impossible possible.

This book is your invitation to do the same...

The Hidden Power Within

We live in a world that often feels chaotic and beyond our control. There are societal expectations, economic pressures, and personal challenges that seem to dictate the course of our lives. It's easy to feel like a victim of circumstance, to believe that life happens to us rather than for us. But what if the true power lies not in the external world but within your own mind?

What if I told you that your thoughts, beliefs, and emotions are the most potent tools you have to create the life you desire? This might sound like a bold statement, but it's grounded in principles that have been studied and practiced for centuries. From ancient wisdom to modern science, the evidence is clear: the mind is not just a passive observer of reality. It's a powerful creator.

Think about it—everything you see around you was once an idea in someone's mind. The chair you're sitting on, the phone in your hand, the home you live in—all of these began as thoughts, ideas that were brought into the physical world through action and belief. The same principle applies to your life. Your current reality is a reflection of your past thoughts, beliefs, and actions. And if you want to change your reality, you must start by changing your thoughts.

The Genie in Your Mind

Picture this: you stumble upon an ancient lamp, and as you rub it, a Genie appears, offering to grant you three wishes. The catch? These wishes are limited only by your imagination. Now, imagine that this Genie isn't a mystical creature but a metaphor for your mind. Just as the Genie has the power to make your wishes come true, your mind has the power to manifest your deepest desires.

But there's a twist—while the Genie in the stories is bound by the commands of its master, your mind is bound only by the limits you impose on it. The number of wishes isn't capped at three; it's infinite. Your mind is always at work, shaping your experiences, your opportunities, and your reality based on the thoughts and beliefs you feed it.

The problem is that most of us are unaware of this power. We let our minds run on autopilot, driven by fear, doubt, and limiting beliefs. We focus on what we don't want, on our worries and insecurities, and in doing so, we inadvertently attract more of the same. The Genie—your mind—responds to the energy you project, whether it's positive or negative, and brings it into your life.

But here's the good news: you can take control. You can become the master of your mind, guiding it to create the life you've always wanted. And this book will show you how.

Manifestation has often been relegated to the realm of the "woo-woo" spiritual world, misunderstood as something mystical or unattainable. But the truth is, we are all manifesting things into our lives every second, whether we realize it or not. Our thoughts, emotions, and beliefs are constantly shaping our reality. Manifestation isn't just about wishing for something and waiting for it to appear; it's about recognizing that the energy we put out into the world is continuously drawing similar energy back to us. Whether you're conscious of it or not, you're always creating your experience through the thoughts you entertain and the beliefs you hold. Understanding this truth is the key to unlocking your potential and deliberately manifesting the life you desire.

The Journey Ahead

In the chapters that follow, you will embark on a journey to unlock the full potential of your mind. You will learn how to harness the power of your thoughts and beliefs to manifest your dream life. You'll discover how to break free from limiting beliefs that have held you back, and how to replace them with empowering ones that propel you forward. You'll explore the transformative power of positive affirmations, the importance of setting clear intentions, and the art of visualizing your success.

But this journey isn't just about learning new techniques or adopting a positive mindset. It's about fundamentally shifting the way you see yourself and the world around you. It's about realizing that you are the creator of your reality, not a passive participant in it. It's about stepping into your power and reclaiming the magic that has always been within you.

As you read, you might find yourself questioning old assumptions, challenging deeply ingrained beliefs, and stepping out of your comfort zone. This is all part of the process. Change is rarely easy, but it is always worth it. And as you begin to see the results of your new mindset—whether it's attracting new opportunities, improving your relationships, or achieving goals that once seemed out of reach—you'll understand just how powerful this journey can be.

Your Life, Your Creation

By the time you finish this book, you'll have a deep understanding of the principles that govern the art of manifestation. More importantly, you'll have the tools to apply these principles to your own life. You'll be equipped to transform your thoughts into tangible results, to turn your dreams into reality, and to live a life that truly reflects your highest potential.

But remember, knowledge alone isn't enough. The real magic happens when you put these principles into practice, when you take action with the belief that you are capable of achieving anything you set your mind to. This book will guide you every step of the way, but it's up to you to take that first step.

So, are you ready to unlock the magic within? Are you ready to become the master of your mind and the creator of your reality? If so, then let's begin this journey together.

Your dream life is waiting, and the power to create it is already within you. All you need to do is believe.

The True Story of Aladdin and his Lamp

Let me start off by explaining the real story of Aladdin and his lamp. The story you know today was based on a real-life event but was changed into a fairytale to make it more accessible for children. A long time ago, around the year 1300

AD, there was a young man named Musa. He lived in a city near Baghdad and was very poor. Despite his kind heart, Musa was so desperate for food and money that he turned to a life of crime, stealing small things to survive.

One day, Musa met a group of thieves who promised him a share of a big treasure if he helped them. They told Musa about a hidden cave filled with gold and jewels which belonged to a local merchant, but the entrance was very small. Since Musa was the smallest among them, they persuaded him to go inside and collect the treasure for them.

Excited by the chance to finally have enough money, Musa agreed. He crawled into the cave and found the treasure, just as the thieves had said. He gathered as much as he could and handed it through the entrance to the thieves. But as soon as they had all the treasure, the thieves betrayed Musa and left him trapped inside the cave.

Feeling hopeless and scared, Musa tried everything to escape, but the entrance was too small to get out on his own. Exhausted and desperate, Musa eventually fell into a comatose state. In his sleep, he had a vivid dream, almost like a vision. In this dream, a wise figure appeared to him. It told Musa that the real power to change his life wasn't in the treasure, but within himself. He encouraged Musa to believe in his own strength and wisdom.

When Musa woke up, dehydrated and close to death, he felt a new sense of determination. He carefully examined the cave and found a small opening that led to a narrow tunnel. With great effort and persistence, Musa managed to squeeze through and find his way out. He emerged from the cave tired but filled with hope and a new understanding of his own abilities.

Musa decided to change his ways. He used the small amount of treasure he had hidden in his pockets to start a new, honest life. He helped his community, gaining the respect and admiration of the people. He built up a small merchant business which eventually turned into a huge success where he became extremely wealthy. As soon as he earnt his riches, the first deed Musa carried out was to repay the merchant whose cave he had helped rob years before.

His kindness and wisdom soon reached the ears of the ruling Sultan, who was impressed by Musa's character so made Musa second in command. Over time, Musa's reputation for fairness and leadership grew, and when the old

Sultan went on an expedition, never to return, the people chose Musa to be their new leader. As Sultan, Musa ruled with compassion and justice. He always remembered the lesson he learned in the cave: that true power comes from within. Under his leadership, the kingdom prospered, and Musa was loved throughout the land.

As you can see from this story Musa's ability to escape the cave and transform his life shows that true strength and power come from within. Even when faced with betrayal and hardship, Musa's determination helped him overcome obstacles. The Genie that has been depicted in the fairytale was simply the power of Musa's mind that helped him to make all his dreams come true. And like Musa, you too have the ability to do this in your life.

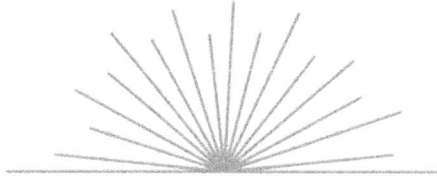

Chapter 2

Your Two Minds—The Conscious and Subconscious

You might wonder how it's possible to have a "Genie" inside you that can grant wishes. The answer lies in understanding how your mind works, particularly the dynamic between your conscious and subconscious mind.

The Conscious Mind is the part of your brain you're most aware of. It's where your thoughts, decisions, and actions take place. This is the part of your mind that decides what to focus on, what goals to pursue, and what plans to make. Think of it as the captain of a ship, steering your life in the direction you choose.

The Subconscious Mind operates behind the scenes, like the crew members of the ship. It handles all the automatic functions of your body—your heartbeat, breathing, and even your emotions and memories. It's a storehouse of everything you've experienced, learned, and felt throughout your life. The subconscious mind is incredibly powerful, influencing your behaviors and reactions often without you even realizing it.

While the conscious mind is responsible for decision-making, the subconscious mind makes those decisions a reality by driving your actions, habits, and beliefs. Together, these two aspects of your mind form a powerful team. But to unlock the full potential of your subconscious mind, you need to learn how to guide it effectively.

An Idyllic Day in July: A Road Trip through Different Lenses

On the most idyllic day in July, when the air was warm and filled with the scent of summer, four friends set off on a road trip around the most picturesque towns known to man. Their journey was meant to be a delightful escape—a chance to connect, explore, and immerse themselves in the charm of small towns that looked like something straight out of a travel magazine. The sun hung high in the sky, casting a golden glow over the landscape as they wound through narrow roads surrounded by rolling hills, lush vineyards, and towering mountains that tumbled down to meet the emerald sea.

As the day drew to a close, the sun dipped toward the horizon, bathing everything in shades of pink and orange. They found themselves driving through a boutique town perched on the side of a winding mountain road. The town overlooked the shimmering waters of the Mediterranean, with quaint cobblestone streets, cosy cafés, and elegant shops lining its main avenue. The scene was like a postcard come to life: terracotta rooftops, whitewashed walls covered in bougainvillea, and the distant sound of waves lapping gently against the rocky shore.

But as picturesque as it was, the four friends, though sharing the same physical space and witnessing the same scenery, each experienced this moment in radically different ways.

Passenger 1: The Driver's Tension

Jennifer, who was driving, felt none of the peace and beauty that the others might have seen. Her hands gripped the steering wheel tightly, her knuckles pale as her mind was consumed with one singular thought: *Where's the next petrol station?*

As the winding road snaked its way along the cliffside, Jennifer kept glancing down at the fuel gauge. It was hovering just above a quarter tank, but out here, in this unfamiliar place with no sign of the nearest service station, her anxiety flared. Every time they passed a road sign, her eyes scanned for a hint of where she could fill up. But all she saw were directions to nearby villages, scenic lookouts, and recommendations for local wines.

The view, though stunning, didn't register with her. The sight of the picturesque town with its charming boutiques and happy locals was blurred by her racing thoughts. In her mind, all she could picture was the car stuttering to a halt on the side of a lonely road, far from help. How long would it take for someone to come? Would they have to call for roadside assistance? What if there was no signal?

Her muscles were tense, and her heart pounded with a steady rhythm of worry. Every twist in the road, every glance at the setting sun only added to the stress. The sinking light meant that soon it would be dark, and the idea of being stranded at night in a foreign place filled her with dread.

The others in the car might have been relaxed, enjoying the ride, but for Jennifer, this moment was anything but idyllic. She longed for the relief of seeing a petrol station sign—something mundane, something that would pull her out of her spiraling anxiety and allow her to focus on enjoying the trip as she had intended. But until then, she was locked in her own mental prison, unable to fully appreciate the world outside.

Passenger 2: The Envy of Luxury

In the passenger seat beside Jennifer sat Lia, who had her eyes glued to the scene outside, but her focus was far from the natural beauty of the town or the ocean beyond. Her attention was drawn entirely to the boutiques lining the streets and the people sauntering along the sidewalks, shopping bags swinging from their arms.

She watched as a couple, both dressed in designer clothes, stepped out of an upscale jewelry store, laughing and holding hands. Behind them, a group of young women emerged from a high-end clothing boutique, their hands full of branded shopping bags, chatting excitedly as they admired each other's purchases. Their clothes were perfectly fitted, their hair styled in a way that spoke of effortless wealth, and everything about them screamed privilege and comfort.

Lia's stomach twisted with envy. Her own clothes were worn from seasons of repeated use, her shoes practical rather than stylish, and her wallet light from too many compromises. She knew it was silly to feel this way, but she couldn't help it. These people seemed to live in a different world—one where money was never a concern, where every desire could be satisfied with a swipe of a card. The luxury on display, from the gleaming watches in the store windows to the sleek cars parked along the curb, made her feel small and insignificant.

As they drove past the boutiques, Lia imagined what it would be like to be one of those women—carefree, financially secure, and adorned in the finest clothes and accessories. She fantasized about walking into one of those stores and buying whatever she wanted without checking the price tag. But that wasn't her reality, and the gap between what she longed for and what she had felt like an unbridgeable chasm.

While Jennifer worried about petrol, Lia's mind was filled with a different kind of emptiness—one marked by a sense of lack and longing. The beauty of the town was overshadowed by the ache of desire and the pangs of jealousy that gnawed at her insides.

Passenger 3: Lost in the Digital World

In the back seat, Lottie was barely aware of her surroundings. Her face was illuminated by the glow of her phone screen, her fingers dancing over the keyboard as she scrolled through social media and replied to messages. The real world outside the car window was a blur—she was deep within the confines of the digital realm, where notifications, likes, and comments demanded her attention.

Lottie had been snapping photos earlier in the trip, but now those moments were being filtered, edited, and shared with her followers. She was meticulously crafting captions, curating her feed, and keeping track of how many likes each post garnered. As the car wound through the charming town, she hardly lifted her eyes from the screen. The sunset outside, with its blazing colors and dramatic reflections on the sea, was missed entirely, replaced by the artificial light of her phone.

Messages from friends popped up, drawing her into conversations that had nothing to do with where she was. Someone was talking about plans for the weekend, another was complaining about a recent breakup, and yet another was sharing memes and jokes. The constant buzz of the digital world kept her mind engaged, even as the present moment slipped away unnoticed.

To Lottie, the road trip was just another backdrop for content. She was vaguely aware that they were somewhere beautiful, but the details were lost on her. She didn't really see the boutiques or the charming architecture or the people enjoying their evening strolls. The journey, the scenery, and even the company of her friends became secondary to the endless stream of online interactions that consumed her attention.

Passenger 4: Finding Joy in the Moment

In stark contrast to the others, Isla, sitting quietly beside Lottie, was fully immersed in the experience. She leaned her head against the window, a content smile playing on her lips as she soaked in the sights and sounds of the quaint town. The air was crisp and carried a faint scent of the sea, which grew stronger when she rolled down her window. The breeze brushed across her face, bringing with it a sense of freedom and tranquility.

As the sun dipped lower, casting long shadows and painting the sky with shades of pink, orange, and deep blue, Isla felt a surge of gratitude wash over her. She could hear the distant murmur of laughter from the café terraces where friends gathered to share a meal. The sight of locals strolling through the town, their faces relaxed and joyful, brought a warmth to her heart.

Her eyes wandered from the charming cobblestone streets to the view of the ocean beyond, where the waves sparkled like diamonds in the fading light. The town was alive with a gentle buzz, a hum of life that was vibrant yet peaceful. Isla felt connected to it all—the scenery, the people, the very air around her. In this moment, she was truly present, savoring every detail, every sensation.

While the others were caught up in their own worlds—worry, envy, distraction—Isla found herself enveloped in a sense of wonder. She felt fortunate to be here, to witness this beauty, and to share it with her friends, even if they didn't seem to notice it the way she did. The scene before her was more than just a pretty view; it was a reminder of the simple joys in life and the peace that comes from embracing the present.

As the car moved forward, carrying them out of the town and back onto the open road, Isla closed her eyes and took a deep breath, holding onto the sense of calm and fulfilment that the moment had given her. For her, this road trip was everything she had hoped it would be—a journey not just through beautiful places, but through the beauty of simply being alive.

Four Perspectives, One Experience

Though the four friends were all in the same car, traveling the same route, their experiences could not have been more different. Jennifer's focus on fuel turned the trip into a stressful task; Lia's envy clouded her ability to appreciate the beauty around her; Lottie's immersion in her digital world made her oblivious to the real world; and Isla, in her mindfulness, found joy and gratitude in the moment.

Their journey reminds us that our perception shapes our reality. Beauty, peace, stress, and longing are all born from within. The world outside is the same for everyone, but what we bring to it—our thoughts, emotions, and focus— creates vastly different experiences. As the car continued down the winding road, one could only wonder how the next stop on their journey would be perceived through each of their unique lenses.

This story highlights a fundamental truth about human experience: while we may share the same physical surroundings or events, each person's internal world shapes how they perceive and react to those experiences. Here's a deeper exploration of this idea:

1. The Lens of Subjectivity:

Imagine a group of people standing side by side, looking at the same painting. While the image is objectively the same, each person will interpret it differently based on their own unique background. Some may focus on the colors, others on the emotions it evokes, and some may even project personal memories onto it. In this sense, our minds act like filters, and everything we perceive passes through these filters. These filters are shaped by our past experiences, beliefs, cultural conditioning, and expectations.

In the road trip story, each passenger's experience of the same scene was drastically different because they all carried different mental lenses. The driver's lens was shaped by anxiety and responsibility, turning the scene into a source of stress. The second passenger's lens was shaped by feelings of inadequacy and longing, causing her to see lack rather than beauty. The third passenger's lens was entirely inward-focused, lost in the digital world and missing the present moment. And the fourth passenger's lens was one of appreciation and mindfulness, allowing her to fully immerse herself in the beauty of the moment.

This illustrates how, even when we are in the exact same place and situation, what we experience is not merely "what's out there" but what our mind creates based on its own internal landscape.

2. The Illusion of Objectivity:

It's easy to assume that our perception of reality is accurate, that what we see and feel is an objective reflection of the world. However, the truth is that reality is colored by the stories we tell ourselves, our past traumas or joys, our deepest fears and desires. For instance, someone who has experienced betrayal might approach relationships with suspicion, even if there's no immediate reason to be distrustful. Their perception of others is filtered through past pain.

This is why two people can have completely different interpretations of the same situation. One person may see a rainy day as dreary and depressing, while another sees it as cozy and refreshing. It's not the external event—the rain—that determines their mood, but the internal story each person holds about what rain means to them.

3. The Trap of External Control:

Many people believe that if they could just change their external circumstances—get a better job, move to a nicer place, find the right partner—they would be happier. But this approach often leads to a cycle of chasing temporary fixes. Even when those changes are made, dissatisfaction eventually returns, because the underlying issues remain unresolved. The real source of our contentment or discontent lies within, not outside.

This is why the statement suggests that we need to "stop thinking we need to change what's out there." The world outside is largely beyond our control, and constantly trying to mold it to our preferences only leads to frustration. Instead, the key to lasting peace and happiness lies in transforming our internal world—our thoughts, beliefs, and perceptions.

4. As Within, So Without:

This ancient principle speaks to the idea that our outer reality is a reflection of our inner state. When we cultivate a sense of inner peace, gratitude, and acceptance, our experience of the external world shifts accordingly. We begin to notice beauty where we once saw only flaws, and we respond to challenges with resilience rather than stress. If our inner world is filled with negativity, fear, or bitterness, those emotions will color everything we perceive.

The concept of "as within, so without" is also tied to the idea of manifestation. The energy we project through our thoughts and emotions tends to attract similar energy from the world around us. For example, a person who carries an attitude of scarcity may find themselves constantly facing financial struggles, even when they have opportunities for abundance. On the other hand, someone who cultivates an attitude of gratitude may find that life offers them more reasons to be grateful.

5. Inner Work: The Path to True Change:

True change starts from within. Rather than seeking to control or manipulate the outside world, focusing on inner transformation allows us to approach life from a place of peace, clarity, and empowerment. Inner work might involve healing past wounds, challenging limiting beliefs, or simply practicing mindfulness and gratitude. When we change our internal state, the world doesn't necessarily change—what changes is how we relate to it.

This doesn't mean that the external world is irrelevant. We still need to take action and make decisions based on our circumstances. However, when our internal world is grounded and aligned, those actions and decisions come from a place of clarity and wisdom rather than fear or reaction. In the road trip scenario, if the driver had been more centered, she might have approached the fuel situation calmly, trusting that a solution would present itself rather than spiraling into anxiety. The second passenger might have been able to appreciate the town's charm rather than feeling inadequate, and the third passenger might have put down her phone and allowed herself to fully experience the moment.

6. The Practice of Mindfulness and Presence

One of the most effective ways to align our inner and outer worlds is through mindfulness—being fully present in the moment without judgment. When we practice mindfulness, we become aware of our internal dialogue and can begin to see how it shapes our experience. We notice when we're getting caught up in worry, envy, or distraction, and we can gently guide ourselves back to the present.

Presence allows us to experience life more fully, without the filters of past conditioning or future anxieties. It's in the present moment that we can truly connect with the beauty of the world around us, the people we're with, and the richness of life. For the fourth passenger in the story, it was her ability to be fully present that allowed her to experience the sunset, the sea breeze, and the joy of simply being alive.

Conclusion: The World through Our Inner Lens

Ultimately, the world we experience is shaped more by our inner state than by the external circumstances. The same event can be a source of stress for one person, joy for another, or completely irrelevant to someone else—all depending on what's happening inside. By focusing on inner growth, healing, and mindfulness, we can change how we experience the world, leading to greater peace, contentment, and fulfilment.

So, rather than always trying to change what's outside—be it situations, people, or environments—our most powerful tool for transformation lies within ourselves. When we shift our inner world, the outer world will begin to reflect that change back to us.

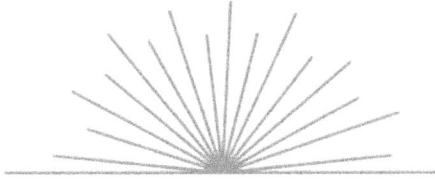

Chapter 3

The Quantum Connection: Science Behind Manifestation

The Marriage of Science and Manifestation

For years, the idea of manifestation has been relegated to the realm of the mystical and the metaphysical, often dismissed as "airy-fairy" by those who prefer concrete evidence. However, in recent decades, science—specifically quantum physics—has begun to uncover principles that resonate deeply with the ancient teachings of manifestation. What was once considered esoteric is now being supported by scientific discoveries that reveal the profound connection between our thoughts, energy, and the reality we experience.

Quantum physics, the branch of science that studies the behavior of particles at the smallest scales of existence, has unveiled a world where the boundaries of reality blur and the observer becomes an integral part of the equation. This chapter explores how the principles of quantum physics align with the concept of manifestation and how understanding these principles can empower you to consciously shape your life.

The Observer Effect: Shaping Reality with Attention

One of the most fascinating discoveries in quantum physics is the observer effect, which suggests that the act of observing a particle can influence its behavior. In experiments, scientists have found that particles such as electrons can exist in multiple states simultaneously, a phenomenon known as superposition. However, when these particles are observed, they "collapse" into a single state or position. This means that the mere act of observation—where you focus your attention—can directly impact the outcome.

This phenomenon has profound implications for the concept of manifestation. If particles, the very building blocks of our reality, respond to observation, then it stands to reason that our thoughts and intentions, when focused, can influence the reality we experience. In essence, what you focus on, you create. The energy you direct towards a particular thought or belief helps to shape and bring it into existence. This idea is at the core of manifestation: by consciously choosing where to direct your attention, you can influence the outcomes in your life.

The Power of Perception: Reality Is What You Make It

The observer effect illustrates a crucial point: reality is not as fixed as we once believed. Instead, it is fluid and malleable, shaped by our perceptions and intentions. Quantum physics challenges the traditional view of a deterministic universe, suggesting that our thoughts and beliefs play an active role in creating our experience of the world.

Consider this: if subatomic particles can be influenced by observation, then our everyday reality, composed of these particles, is also subject to influence by our perceptions. This means that the way we view our circumstances, our potential, and our future can have a tangible impact on what we experience. If you believe that life is full of opportunities, you are likely to notice and attract opportunities. Conversely, if you believe that life is full of obstacles, that belief will shape your experiences accordingly.

Energy and Transformation: The Science of Change

Another key principle of quantum physics is the law of conservation of energy, which states that energy cannot be created or destroyed; it can only be transformed from one form to another. This principle is directly relevant to the process of manifestation. If everything in the universe is made up of energy, and energy is in a constant state of flux, then it follows that we have the power to transform the energy around us to create the reality we desire.

This transformation is not limited to physical energy but also includes the energy of our thoughts, emotions, and beliefs. Negative emotions, such as fear, doubt, and anger, carry a certain frequency of energy. By consciously shifting your focus and changing your thoughts, you can transmute these lower energies into higher frequencies, such as love, confidence, and joy. This process of transmutation is at the heart of manifestation: by changing your internal energy, you change the energy you project into the world, thereby influencing the experiences you attract.

Quantum Entanglement: The Interconnectedness of All Things

Quantum physics also introduces the concept of entanglement, where particles that have interacted with each other remain connected, regardless of the distance separating them. This means that the state of one particle can instantaneously affect the state of another, even if they are light-years apart. This phenomenon suggests a level of interconnectedness that transcends physical boundaries, indicating that everything in the universe is deeply interconnected.

In the context of manifestation, this interconnectedness means that our thoughts and actions are not isolated events. The energy we emit through our thoughts, emotions, and intentions influences not only our immediate environment but also the broader web of existence. By understanding and harnessing this interconnectedness, we can become more deliberate in the energy we project, knowing that it will ripple out and affect the world around us.

Becoming a Conscious Creator

The implications of quantum physics are profound: they suggest that we are not mere bystanders in the universe but active participants in its creation. By understanding that our thoughts and beliefs have the power to shape reality, we can begin to take conscious control of our lives. This means becoming aware of the thoughts we entertain, the emotions we dwell on, and the beliefs we hold, and then choosing to align them with the reality we wish to experience.

Manifestation, then, is not just a mystical concept but a scientifically supported practice of consciously directing energy to create the life you desire. By embracing the principles of quantum physics, you can begin to see yourself as a powerful creator, capable of transforming your reality through the intentional focus of your thoughts and energy.

Conclusion: The Quantum Leap

As we continue to explore the depths of quantum physics, the line between science and spirituality becomes increasingly blurred. The more we learn about the nature of reality at the quantum level, the more we see the truth in ancient teachings about the power of the mind and the energy of thought. Manifestation is no longer just a spiritual practice; it is a scientifically supported process of creation that we engage in every moment of our lives.

By understanding the principles of quantum physics and how they relate to manifestation, you can begin to harness the true power of your mind. You can become a conscious creator, transforming your thoughts and energy to align with the reality you wish to experience. The universe is not a rigid structure, but a dynamic, interconnected field of energy that responds to your focus and intention. By mastering this understanding, you take a quantum leap into a new way of living—one where you are empowered to manifest your dreams and shape your destiny.

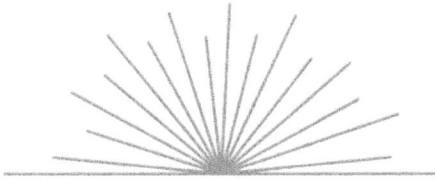

Chapter 4

The World as a Mirror: Reflecting Who We Are and What We Focus On

The world is like a giant mirror, constantly reflecting back to us what we project into it. What we experience in life is a direct reflection of our thoughts, beliefs, emotions, and the energy we carry. This idea—often summarized as "you get what you give" or "what you focus on grows"—speaks to the deep connection between our internal state and the external world. Understanding this concept is key to transforming our reality because it shifts our attention from blaming circumstances to taking responsibility for the energy we bring into the world.

The Law of Attraction and the Power of Focus

At the heart of the idea that the world mirrors us is the law of attraction: the principle that like attracts like. According to this law, our thoughts, feelings, and beliefs emit a vibrational frequency that attracts similar energy back to us. If we're constantly focusing on lack, negativity, or fear, the world tends to mirror those experiences back to us in the form of challenges, setbacks, and difficult situations. On the other hand, if we focus on abundance, gratitude, and positivity, we attract more of those experiences into our lives.

This isn't just about "positive thinking" in a superficial sense. It's about deeply understanding that the world is a reflection of the energy we bring to it. Our focus shapes our reality. If we're always looking for what's wrong or what's missing, that's exactly what we'll keep finding. But when we shift our focus to what's good, to what's possible, and to what we're grateful for, the world begins to reflect that back to us in profound ways.

The Mirror of Relationships: How Others Reflect Us

One of the most powerful ways the world acts as a mirror is through our relationships. The people we encounter—whether they uplift or challenge us—are often reflections of our own internal states. This doesn't mean that we're responsible for other people's behavior, but it does mean that we can learn a lot about ourselves by paying attention to the dynamics in our relationships.

For example, if you find yourself constantly surrounded by people who drain your energy or don't respect you, it's worth examining whether you're holding onto beliefs about being unworthy, disrespected, or powerless. The world is reflecting back to you what you may believe about yourself on a subconscious level. Conversely, if you attract supportive, loving relationships, it's likely because you carry a sense of self-worth and openness to love.

This mirror effect also applies to the traits we notice in others. The qualities that irritate or trigger us in others often point to unresolved issues within ourselves. If someone's arrogance or rudeness gets under your skin, it may be because there's a part of you that either fears those traits or possesses them in a hidden way. On the other hand, when we admire certain qualities in others, it's often because those same traits exist within us, waiting to be more fully expressed.

The world gives us exactly what we need to grow. Every relationship, every interaction, is a reflection that offers us a chance to see ourselves more clearly, heal what needs healing, and elevate what needs to be elevated.

The Feedback Loop: Energy in, Energy Out

The world responds to the energy we put into it. If we approach life with a sense of entitlement, bitterness, or fear, we'll likely find ourselves surrounded by resistance and negativity. However, when we approach life with an attitude of generosity, gratitude, and trust, the world tends to meet us with opportunities, kindness, and support.

This feedback loop is constantly at work. Consider a situation where you wake up in a bad mood, feeling rushed and irritated. As you go through your day, you're more likely to encounter frustrations—like getting stuck in traffic, clashing with colleagues, or facing delays. These external challenges mirror the internal state you started your day with. On the flip side, when you start your day with calmness, positivity, and an intention to embrace whatever comes your way, you'll often find that things flow more smoothly. You're more resilient to challenges, and you're likely to attract positive interactions and outcomes.

This doesn't mean that life will always be easy or that we'll never face challenges. However, when we understand that the energy we bring shapes how we experience the world, we become empowered to shift our focus and, in turn, shift our reality.

Becoming What You Want to Attract

One of the most profound ways to harness the world-as-mirror principle is to embody what you want to attract. If you desire more love, be more loving. If you want more abundance, cultivate a mindset of abundance. If you want more peace, be a source of peace for yourself and others.

The world is not separate from us; it is intricately connected to the energy we carry and the person we choose to be. When we focus on being the kind of person we wish to attract or the kind of energy we wish to experience, the world reflects that back to us. It's as though the mirror says, "Here is what you are being—here it is returned to you."

This approach shifts us from a mindset of scarcity and seeking to one of giving and embodying. Instead of constantly looking for what we can get, we focus on what we can give. And in giving—whether it's kindness, compassion, or positivity—we naturally receive it back, often in greater measure.

The Danger of Focusing on What You Don't Want

The mirror of the world doesn't discriminate between positive and negative energy—it simply reflects whatever you're focused on. This is why it's important to be mindful of where you direct your attention. If you're constantly focused on what's wrong, what you fear, or what you lack, that's what the world will mirror back to you.

For example, if you're always worried about financial scarcity, even if you have enough, you'll continue to experience situations that reinforce that fear. You might miss opportunities, encounter unexpected expenses, or feel constantly stressed about money. The more you focus on what you don't want, the more you inadvertently attract it.

To break this cycle, it's crucial to consciously shift your focus to what you do want—peace, abundance, love, joy. Instead of dwelling on the problems, train yourself to look for solutions, to focus on possibilities, and to maintain a mindset of trust and faith. The more you practice this, the more the world will mirror those positive experiences back to you.

Cultivating Self-Awareness: The Key to Changing the Reflection

The world is always reflecting something back to us, and to fully harness this truth, we need to develop self-awareness. Self-awareness allows us to notice the patterns in our lives and understand how our thoughts, beliefs, and behaviors contribute to what we experience. If you find that certain negative situations keep repeating in your life, it's an opportunity to look within and ask, "What am I projecting that's causing this to show up?"

Changing the reflection requires us to change what's within. This might involve letting go of limiting beliefs, healing past wounds, or shifting from a mindset of fear to one of trust. The work is internal, but the results show up externally. The more you elevate your internal state, the more the world reflects that elevated state back to you.

The Role of Gratitude and Presence

Gratitude and presence are two powerful tools that help us shift our focus and align with what we want the world to reflect back to us. Gratitude shifts our focus from what's missing to what's already good in our lives, creating a sense of abundance. When we focus on what we're grateful for, we attract more reasons to be grateful.

Presence, on the other hand, allows us to experience life as it is rather than through the lens of past pain or future worry. When we're fully present, we engage with the world from a place of clarity and openness, allowing us to see the opportunities, beauty, and goodness that are available right here and now.

Together, gratitude and presence help us stay aligned with the energy we want the world to reflect back to us.

Conclusion: Shaping Your Reality from Within

The world is a mirror, reflecting not just what we think, but who we are being. When we focus on positivity, gratitude, love, and abundance, the world gives those things back to us in kind. When we focus on fear, lack, and negativity, we experience more of those things in our lives. This mirror effect is always at work, shaping our reality based on the energy we project.

By taking responsibility for our thoughts, emotions, and actions, we can consciously shape the reflection we receive. Instead of reacting to what life gives us, we become proactive in creating the life we want by first cultivating it within ourselves. The more we focus on being what we want to experience—peaceful, loving, abundant—the more the world will mirror those qualities back to us.

In the end, the world reflects not just what we focus on, but what we choose to become. By aligning our inner world with the qualities we wish to experience, we take control of our reality and create a life that truly reflects our highest intentions and desires.

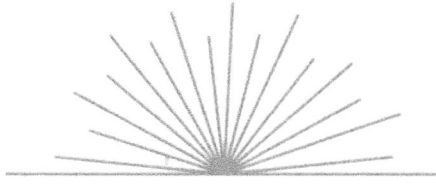

Chapter 5

Disassociation from the Past: Embracing the Present as a New Beginning

The Power of Perception: How Our Past Shapes Our Present

Our experiences shape our perceptions, and our perceptions, in turn, shape our reality. The mind is incredibly powerful; it has the ability to color our present experiences with the hues of our past, often without us even realizing it. When we carry the weight of past experiences into the present, we risk distorting our view of the world, making it difficult to see things as they truly are. This is particularly true when it comes to places, people, or situations that we have strong associations with—either positive or negative. The key to living fully in the present is to disassociate from the past, allowing each moment to be experienced as it truly is, free from the burden of past memories and emotions.

35

The Bowling Alley Analogy: A Tale of Two Perspectives

Imagine two people walking into a bowling alley. On the surface, the bowling alley is just a place—a neutral environment with lanes, pins, balls, and the familiar sounds of bowling balls striking pins. However, the two individuals walking in are carrying with them vastly different perceptions of the place based on their past experiences.

Person One: Haunted by the Past

Person one had a negative experience at this bowling alley years ago. Perhaps they were embarrassed in front of a group of friends, or maybe they received bad news while they were there. The details of the past experience are less important than the emotional imprint it left. As soon as this person steps into the bowling alley, they are filled with a sense of dread and anxiety. Their mind begins to race, replaying the past event in vivid detail. Even though the physical space is the same as it was years ago, their perception of it is anything but neutral.

For this person, the bowling alley is no longer just a place; it has become a trigger for negative thoughts and emotions. The feelings of discomfort and unease they experienced in the past resurface, and they begin to expect the worst. This expectation, born out of past experiences, colors their current reality. They might notice every small annoyance or inconvenience, reinforcing their belief that this place is associated with negative experiences. By carrying the past into the present, they inadvertently attract more negativity, making it difficult to enjoy the moment or see the bowling alley for what it truly is—a neutral environment.

Person Two: Filled with Anticipation

Person two, on the other hand, has only positive memories associated with the bowling alley. Perhaps it was the site of a first date, a fun night out with friends, or a place where they achieved a personal best score. As soon as this person enters the bowling alley, they are filled with a sense of joy and anticipation. Their mind recalls the laughter, the fun, and the sense of accomplishment they experienced in the past. For them, the bowling alley is a place of positivity and enjoyment.

Because their past experiences were positive, person two is likely to approach the present moment with a sense of optimism. They are more likely to notice the pleasant aspects of the environment—the friendly staff, the clean lanes, the upbeat music. This positive outlook creates a feedback loop, where their expectations of a good time are met with experiences that confirm those expectations. In this way, person two's positive past experiences help to create a positive present reality.

The Neutrality of the Present: Disassociating from the Past

The bowling alley itself is neutral. It is not inherently good or bad; it is simply a place. The experiences of the two individuals are shaped not by the place itself, but by the associations they bring with them. This example illustrates a powerful truth: the past only has the power to influence the present if we allow it to.

The challenge is to recognize when our past experiences are coloring our perception of the present and to consciously disassociate from those past experiences. Just because something happened in the past doesn't mean it will happen again. Every moment is a new opportunity, a blank slate, and it is up to us to decide how we will experience it.

The Consequences of Living in the Past

When we allow past experiences to dictate our present, we are not truly living in the moment. Instead, we are trapped in a cycle of re-living old memories, re-feeling old emotions, and re-experiencing old pain. This can lead to a host of negative consequences, including:

1. Heightened Anxiety and Fear

When we carry past traumas or negative experiences into the present, we are more likely to feel anxious and fearful. Our minds are constantly on high alert, anticipating that something bad will happen, just as it did in the past. This anxiety can prevent us from fully engaging with the present moment and enjoying life as it unfolds.

2. Self-Fulfilling Prophecies

If we expect negative experiences, we are more likely to notice and focus on negative aspects of a situation. This focus can create a self-fulfilling prophecy, where our negative expectations lead to negative outcomes. For example, if person one from the bowling alley example expects to have a bad time, they may be more likely to misinterpret neutral or even positive events as negative, thus reinforcing their belief that the place is inherently bad.

3. Missed Opportunities for Growth

When we are stuck in the past, we miss out on the opportunities for growth and change that the present moment offers. Each new experience is an opportunity to learn, grow, and create new, positive memories. However, if we are too focused on past hurts or disappointments, we may be unable to see these opportunities and take advantage of them.

4. Strained Relationships

Living in the past can also strain our relationships with others. If we are constantly replaying old arguments, misunderstandings, or betrayals, we may find it difficult to fully trust or connect with others in the present. This can lead to a sense of isolation and loneliness, as well as difficulty in forming new, healthy relationships.

Strategies for Disassociating from the Past

Disassociating from the past requires conscious effort and practice, but it is entirely possible. By letting go of past experiences and approaching each moment as a new, unique opportunity, we can begin to experience life more fully and authentically. Here are some strategies to help you disassociate from the past and embrace the present:

1. Practice Mindfulness

Mindfulness is the practice of being fully present in the moment, without judgment or distraction. When you are mindful, you are fully engaged with what is happening right now, rather than being caught up in thoughts about the past or worries about the future. By practicing mindfulness, you can train your mind to focus on the present moment and let go of past experiences that no longer serve you.

One way to practice mindfulness is through deep breathing exercises. When you find yourself dwelling on the past, take a few deep breaths, and bring your attention back to the present moment. Focus on the sensations of your breath, the sounds around you, or the physical sensations in your body. This simple practice can help to ground you in the present and reduce the influence of past memories.

2. Reframe Your Thoughts

Cognitive reframing is a technique used to change the way you think about a situation. Instead of seeing the present through the lens of the past, try to see it as a new, separate experience. Ask yourself if there is any real evidence that the past will repeat itself, or if you are simply assuming it will because of your previous experiences.

For example, if you find yourself dreading a visit to a place where you had a negative experience in the past, remind yourself that this is a new day and a new opportunity. The circumstances are different, and you have the power to create a different outcome. By consciously choosing to reframe your thoughts, you can begin to break the cycle of negative associations.

3. Release Emotional Attachments

Our past experiences often carry emotional weight that can keep us tethered to old memories. One way to disassociate from the past is to consciously release these emotional attachments. This might involve forgiving yourself or others for past mistakes, letting go of grudges, or simply acknowledging that the past is over and cannot be changed.

Journaling can be a helpful tool for releasing emotional attachments. Write about your past experiences, how they made you feel, and what you learned from them. Then, write a statement of release, such as "I release this memory and the emotions associated with it. I choose to live fully in the present." This act of writing can help to solidify your intention to let go of the past and move forward.

4. Focus on Positive Present Experiences

One of the best ways to disassociate from the past is to create new, positive experiences in the present. Focus on activities that bring you joy, fulfilment, and a sense of accomplishment. Surround yourself with people who uplift and support you, and seek out environments that make you feel safe and happy.

By consciously choosing to create positive experiences, you can begin to replace old, negative associations with new, positive ones. Over time, these new experiences will help to reshape your perception of the world and reinforce the belief that the present is full of possibilities.

5. Embrace the Unknown

The past often feels familiar, even if it was painful or difficult. The present, on the other hand, is full of unknowns, which can be both exciting and intimidating. To fully disassociate from the past, it is important to embrace the unknown and approach each new experience with curiosity and openness.

Remind yourself that the unknown is not something to be feared, but something to be explored. Each moment is a new opportunity to learn, grow, and create a different future. By embracing the unknown, you free yourself from the constraints of the past and open yourself up to the endless possibilities of the present.

Living Fully in the Present

Disassociating from the past does not mean forgetting or ignoring what has happened. It simply means recognizing that the past is over and no longer has the power to control your present experiences. By letting go of past associations and embracing each moment as a new beginning, you can start to live more fully and authentically.

The key to disassociation from the past is to approach life with a sense of openness and curiosity. Rather than assuming that history will repeat itself, allow yourself to experience the present moment as it truly is—free from the weight of past memories and emotions. Each day is a new opportunity to create the life you want, and the only way to seize that opportunity is to let go of the past and live fully in the present.

So, the next time you walk into a place that holds memories—whether good or bad—remind yourself that this moment is unique. The place is neutral, and it is your perception that will shape your experience. Choose to see the present as a blank slate, and allow yourself to create new, positive memories that will serve you in the future. By doing so, you will not only disassociate from the past but also empower yourself to live a life filled with possibility, joy, and fulfilment.

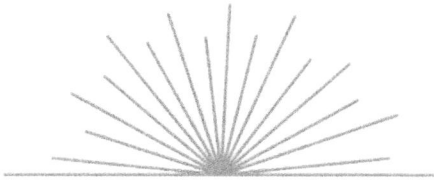

Chapter 6

Understanding and Overcoming Anxiety: The key to Free your Mind

Anxiety is a deeply ingrained part of the human experience, often lurking at the edges of our consciousness, feeding on our fears and uncertainties. It arises when we anticipate potential threats, projecting worst-case scenarios onto the canvas of our future. This constant state of worry can cloud our judgment, hinder our progress, and keep us trapped in a cycle of negativity. But what if you could break free from this cycle? What if you could master the art of taking control of your thoughts, steering them away from fear and towards the creation of a brighter future?

When you learn to harness the power of your mind and direct it towards positive outcomes, the anxiety that once held you back begins to lose its grip.

By assuming control over your thoughts, you're not only shaping your future but also finding relief from the mental and emotional strain that anxiety brings. This newfound peace of mind opens the door to a more fulfilling and empowered life, where you can manifest your desires with clarity and confidence. As you continue to practice these principles, you'll discover that the calm and focus you achieve not only enhance your ability to manifest your dreams but also bring a profound sense of inner peace, making it easier to navigate life's challenges with grace and resilience.

In this chapter, we will explore the impact of anxiety on our lives, delve into practical techniques for managing it, and discuss the importance of support and proper nutrition in overcoming this pervasive emotion.

The Impact of Anxiety

Anxiety is a complex and multifaceted experience, manifesting differently for each person. At its core, anxiety is an evolutionary response—a mechanism designed to keep us safe from harm. In ancient times, our ancestors relied on this heightened state of alertness to avoid predators and other dangers. However, in the modern world, where physical threats are less common, anxiety has morphed into a more pervasive and sometimes debilitating condition.

The primary source of anxiety is fear—specifically, fear of the unknown and the future. This fear often takes the form of overthinking, where the mind fixates on potential negative outcomes, spiraling into a cycle of worry and dread. For instance, someone might be anxious about an upcoming job interview, fearing they will say the wrong thing or fail to impress the interviewer. Although these fears are often irrational and disproportionate to the actual risk, they can feel overwhelming and all-consuming.

Anxiety can have profound effects on both the mind and body. Mentally, it can lead to persistent worry, difficulty concentrating, and a sense of impending doom. Physically, it can manifest as a racing heart, shortness of breath, muscle tension, and even gastrointestinal issues. Over time, chronic anxiety can contribute to more serious health problems, such as heart disease, high blood pressure, and weakened immune function.

The negative thought cycle that fuels anxiety is particularly insidious. It often begins with a single worry—perhaps about an uncertain outcome. This worry then triggers a cascade of related concerns, each building on the last until the individual is trapped in a loop of anxiety and fear. For example, a person might start by worrying about a presentation at work. This worry might then lead to thoughts about losing their job, financial instability, and the impact on their family, creating a snowball effect that magnifies the original concern.

Breaking free from this cycle requires disrupting the negative thought patterns that sustain anxiety. This can be achieved through a combination of mindfulness, awareness, and proactive mental exercises designed to reframe one's thinking and foster a more balanced perspective.

Techniques to Manage Anxiety

Managing anxiety is a journey that requires patience, persistence, and self-compassion. While anxiety cannot always be eliminated, it can be managed effectively with the right strategies. Below are some techniques that can help individuals cope with and reduce their anxiety:

Mindfulness and Awareness

Again, Mindfulness can support you with this at is enables you to practice being fully present in the moment, without judgment or distraction. It involves paying attention to one's thoughts, feelings, and physical sensations with an open and accepting attitude. By cultivating mindfulness, individuals can become more aware of their anxiety triggers and learn to respond to them in healthier ways.

When anxiety arises, it often comes with a flurry of negative thoughts. These thoughts can feel automatic and uncontrollable, but with mindfulness, it's possible to observe them without getting caught up in them. For example, if someone feels anxious about a social event, they might notice thoughts like "What if I embarrass myself?" or "Everyone will think I'm awkward." Instead of reacting to these thoughts with more anxiety, they can acknowledge them as just thoughts—temporary mental events that do not necessarily reflect reality.

Practicing mindfulness can help individuals break the cycle of negative thinking by creating a space between the stimulus (the anxious thought) and the response (the feeling of anxiety). This space allows for greater clarity and choice in how to respond. Techniques such as deep breathing, progressive muscle relaxation, and guided imagery can also be incorporated into a mindfulness practice to further reduce anxiety.

Reading: Uplifting and Empowering Literature

Books have the power to transport us to different worlds, offering a temporary escape from the stresses and worries of everyday life. Reading can be a particularly effective tool for managing anxiety, as it engages the mind and provides a distraction from anxious thoughts.

However, not all reading material is created equal when it comes to managing anxiety. It is important to choose books that are uplifting, empowering, and aligned with personal values and goals. Fictional stories with positive themes, self-help books that offer practical advice, and biographies of individuals who have overcome adversity can all provide inspiration and encouragement.

For example, reading about someone who has successfully navigated challenges similar to one's own can foster a sense of hope and possibility. Similarly, engaging with stories that emphasize resilience, courage, and personal growth can reinforce positive thinking patterns and reduce feelings of helplessness.

Incorporating regular reading into one's routine can also serve as a form of self-care, offering a respite from the demands of daily life. Setting aside time each day to read—whether in the morning, during a lunch break, or before bed—can create a soothing ritual that promotes relaxation and mental well-being.

Music and Dance: Shifting Mood and Perspective

Music has a profound impact on our emotions and can be a powerful tool for managing anxiety. Listening to music that is uplifting, soothing, or energizing can significantly alter one's mood and perspective. The rhythm, melody, and lyrics of a song can evoke positive emotions, trigger memories, and even change the way we perceive a situation.

For example, listening to a favorite song or playlist can provide a sense of comfort and familiarity, helping to counteract feelings of anxiety. Upbeat music can also boost energy levels and motivation, making it easier to tackle tasks that might otherwise feel overwhelming.

Dance, too, is an effective way to manage anxiety. Moving the body to music not only releases physical tension but also helps channel emotional energy in a positive direction. Dance allows for self-expression and creativity, providing an outlet for emotions that might otherwise be difficult to articulate.

Engaging in dance, whether alone or with others, can create a sense of connection and joy, which are powerful antidotes to anxiety. Even a few minutes of dancing each day can make a noticeable difference in one's mood and overall sense of well-being.

The Importance of Support and Nutrition

Overcoming anxiety is not a solitary endeavor. It requires the support of others and a commitment to overall well-being, including proper nutrition. In this section, we will explore the role of social support and nutrition in managing anxiety.

Seeking Support from Loved Ones

One of the most effective ways to combat anxiety is to seek support from loved ones. Anxiety often thrives in isolation, feeding off the belief that one is alone in their struggles. However, reaching out to others can break this isolation and provide a sense of connection and understanding.

Talking to someone about what you're experiencing can be incredibly therapeutic. Whether it's a friend, family member, or therapist, sharing your thoughts and feelings can help lighten the emotional burden of anxiety. Others can offer a different perspective, provide reassurance, and remind you that you are not alone in your journey.

In addition to emotional support, loved ones can also offer practical help. For example, they might accompany you to appointments, help you manage responsibilities, or simply spend time with you doing activities that bring you joy. The presence of a supportive person can be a powerful source of comfort and strength, helping to reduce feelings of anxiety and depression.

It is important to remember that asking for help is not a sign of weakness; rather, it is a sign of strength and self-awareness. By acknowledging that you need support, you are taking an important step toward healing and recovery.

The Role of Nutrition in Mental Health

Nutrition plays a critical role in mental health, and certain deficiencies can contribute to symptoms of anxiety and depression. The brain, like any other organ in the body, requires specific nutrients to function optimally. When the body is deficient in these nutrients, it can lead to imbalances that affect mood, energy levels, and overall mental well-being.

For example, Vitamin D is essential for brain health, and a deficiency in this vitamin has been linked to an increased risk of depression and anxiety. Vitamin D is primarily obtained through sunlight exposure, but it can also be found in foods such as fatty fish, fortified dairy products, and eggs.

Iron is another important nutrient for mental health. Iron deficiency can lead to anemia which is associated with fatigue, irritability, and difficulty concentrating—all of which can exacerbate anxiety. Foods rich in iron include red meat, poultry, beans, lentils, and spinach.

Vitamin B12 is crucial for the production of neurotransmitters, the chemicals in the brain that regulate mood. A deficiency in B12 can lead to symptoms of depression and anxiety. Sources of B12 include meat, fish, eggs, and dairy products.

In addition to these specific nutrients, a balanced diet that includes a variety of fruits, vegetables, whole grains, lean proteins, and healthy fats is essential for overall mental health. Eating a diet rich in these foods can help stabilize blood sugar levels, reduce inflammation, and support the production of mood-regulating hormones.

In contrast, a diet high in processed foods, sugar, and unhealthy fats can contribute to anxiety by causing blood sugar spikes and crashes, increasing inflammation, and disrupting hormone balance. Therefore, making conscious food choices and prioritizing nutrition can have a significant impact on managing anxiety.

Conclusion

Understanding and overcoming anxiety is a multifaceted process that involves addressing both the mind and body. By recognizing the impact of anxiety, implementing techniques to manage it, and seeking support and proper nutrition, individuals can take meaningful steps toward reducing their anxiety and improving their overall well-being.

Anxiety may be a persistent part of the human experience, but it does not have to define or control your life. With mindfulness, self-care, and the support of loved ones, it is possible to break free from its grip and reclaim a sense of peace and empowerment.

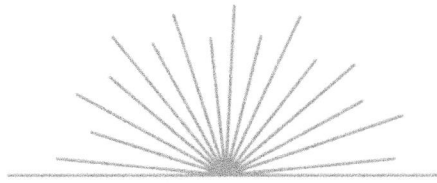

Chapter 7

Understanding the Cognitive Behavioral Therapy (CBT) Cycle

Another useful tool to help alleviate anxiety in our everyday life is Cognitive Behavioral Therapy (CBT). CBT is a powerful approach that focuses on understanding the intricate connections between our thoughts, feelings, behaviors, and physical reactions. The CBT cycle illustrates how these components are interrelated and influence each other in a continuous loop. By changing one component, we can create positive changes in the others, which is the core concept of CBT.

The CBT Cycle: An Overview

At the heart of the CBT model is the belief that our thoughts significantly impact our emotions, behaviors, and even physical responses. The cycle can be broken down into four main components:

1. Thoughts: These are the perceptions and beliefs we hold about ourselves, others, and the world around us. Thoughts can be automatic and are often shaped by our past experiences and current circumstances.

2. Feelings: Our thoughts directly influence our emotional responses. For example, a negative thought such as "I'm not good enough" can lead to feelings of sadness or anxiety.

3. Behaviors: The way we feel affects how we act. Negative emotions can lead to behaviors such as avoidance, procrastination, or even aggression.

4. Physical Reactions: Our body responds to our emotions and thoughts. For instance, anxiety can cause physical symptoms like a racing heart, sweating, or a tight chest.

These four components are interconnected, creating a cycle that can either be positive or negative. When trapped in a negative CBT cycle, an individual might experience a downward spiral where negative thoughts lead to negative feelings, behaviors, and physical symptoms, which then reinforce the negative thoughts. The goal of CBT is to intervene in this cycle by identifying and challenging negative thoughts, thereby altering the resulting feelings, behaviors, and physical reactions.

Breaking the Negative Cycle

To break the negative CBT cycle, it's essential to first become aware of the thoughts that trigger it. This involves paying close attention to the automatic thoughts that arise in response to different situations. Once these thoughts are identified, they can be challenged and reframed into more positive or realistic ones.

CBT Cycle: Thoughts, Feelings, Behaviors, Physical Reactions

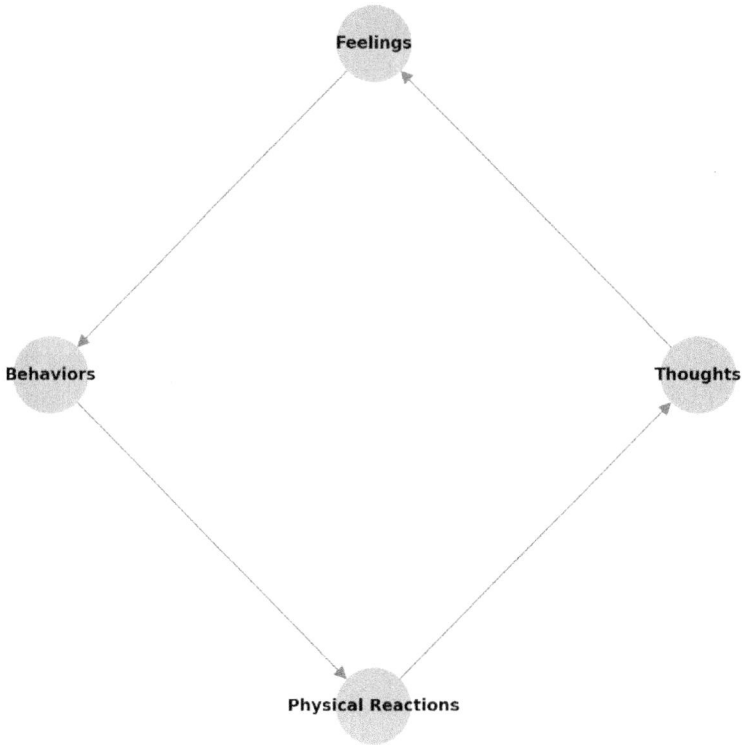

For example, consider someone who thinks, "I'm going to fail this test." This thought might lead to feelings of anxiety, causing them to avoid studying (behavior) and experience physical symptoms like headaches or nausea. By challenging this thought, perhaps by considering past successes or acknowledging the effort put into studying, the person can reframe it to, "I've prepared well, and I'll do my best." This new thought can lead to feelings of calm, behaviors such as focused study, and reduced physical symptoms.

Shifting Your Thought Patterns: Tools for Lasting Change

At the end of our journey through Cognitive Behavioral Therapy (CBT), it's essential to recognize that our thought patterns significantly influence our emotional and mental well-being. By becoming aware of these patterns and actively working to change them, we can create lasting, positive change in our lives. Below are some common thought habits that might be holding you back, along with strategies to reframe them for better mental health:

1. **All-or-Nothing-Thinking**

   Often referred to as "black-and-white" thinking, this pattern involves seeing things in extremes, with no middle ground. For example, you might think, "If I'm not perfect, I'm a complete failure." To counter this, try to recognize the shades of grey in your experiences. Ask yourself, "Is there a more balanced way to view this situation?"

2. **Overgeneralization**

   This habit occurs when you make broad conclusions based on a single event, such as thinking, "I always mess up," after making a mistake. Instead, focus on the specific situation at hand and remind yourself that one instance doesn't define you. Consider asking, "Is it fair to say that this one event represents my entire experience?"

3. **Mental Filtering**

   Mental filtering is the tendency to focus on the negative aspects of a situation while ignoring the positives. This can lead to a distorted view of reality, where only the bad is acknowledged. To break this habit, consciously practice looking for the good in each situation. Ask yourself, "What positives am I overlooking?"

4. **Disqualifying the Positive**

    Even when something good happens, you might dismiss it as a fluke or unimportant, thinking, "That doesn't count because..." Instead of discounting positive experiences, try to acknowledge and appreciate them fully. Ask yourself, "What if I allowed myself to accept this as a genuine success?"

5. **Jumping to Conclusions**

    There are two common forms of this thought pattern: mind-reading and fortune-telling. Mind-reading involves assuming you know what others are thinking, while fortune-telling is about predicting negative outcomes. To challenge this, consider the evidence for your assumptions and ask, "Do I really know this for sure?" or "What are the alternative possibilities?"

6. **Catastrophizing**

    This involves expecting the worst-case scenario to happen, even if it's unlikely. When you notice this pattern, try to evaluate the situation more realistically. Ask yourself, "What's the most likely outcome?" and "How would I cope if the worst did happen?"

7. **Emotional Reasoning**

    Emotional reasoning is when you believe that your feelings reflect reality. For example, "I feel anxious, so something must be wrong." While emotions are important, they are not always accurate indicators of truth. Practice separating your feelings from the facts by asking, "Is my emotion reflecting the reality of the situation?"

8. **"Should" Statements**

These are rigid rules you set for yourself, such as "I should always be productive" or "I shouldn't feel this way." When you catch yourself using "should" statements, consider if they are helpful or realistic. Reframe them as preferences rather than obligations, like "I'd prefer to be productive, but it's okay to rest."

By identifying and challenging these thought patterns, you can begin to change the way you perceive and respond to the world. Over time, with practice and persistence, you'll find that these healthier thinking habits lead to greater emotional resilience and a more balanced life. Remember, the key to lasting change is not just recognizing these patterns, but actively working to reframe and replace them with more constructive ways of thinking.

Who Is in Your Circle?

The people you surround yourself with also play a significant role in shaping your thoughts, behaviors, and overall mental well-being. Your social circle can either uplift and support you or drag you down into negativity.

Positive Influences in Your Circle

Positive individuals are those who make you feel good about yourself and life in general. They have healthy thought patterns, which manifest in their ability to see things from different perspectives, offer support without judgment, and celebrate others' successes without feeling threatened. These individuals contribute to a positive atmosphere where everyone can thrive.

When you're around people who have a balanced and optimistic outlook, you're more likely to adopt similar thought patterns. Their positivity can help you challenge and reframe your own negative thoughts, leading to a healthier CBT cycle.

For example, if you're feeling down about a work setback, a positive friend might remind you of your past achievements or encourage you to view the setback as a learning opportunity. This kind of support can help you shift your thoughts, leading to better emotional and behavioral outcomes.

Negative Influences in Your Circle

Spending time with people who are stuck in negative thought patterns can have the opposite effect. These individuals might focus on their problems, blame others, get easily offended and struggle to see things from different perspectives. Their negativity can be contagious, pulling you into a similar mindset.

If you constantly hear complaints, criticisms, or pessimistic views from those around you, it's challenging to maintain a positive outlook. Over time, this can lead to a negative CBT cycle, where your thoughts, feelings, and behaviors mirror the negativity in your environment.

For example, if you're around someone who always focuses on the negatives of a situation, you might start to do the same. This can lead to feelings of hopelessness, behaviors such as withdrawal or procrastination, and physical symptoms like fatigue or tension.

Evaluating and Adjusting Your Social Circle

To maintain a healthy mindset, it's crucial to evaluate the influence of those in your social circle. Are they supportive and positive, or do they drain your energy with negativity? While it's impossible to avoid all negativity, being mindful of who you spend the most time with can help you create a more positive environment for yourself.

If you find that certain individuals consistently bring negativity into your life, it might be time to set boundaries or reduce your time with them. Surrounding yourself with positive, supportive people can make a significant difference in your mental health and overall well-being.

Time to Make a Change

Recognizing the need for change is the first step towards improving your mental health and overall quality of life. If you find yourself stuck in negative thought patterns or surrounded by negativity, it's time to take action and make positive changes.

The Power of Self-Awareness

Change begins with self-awareness. This involves taking an honest look at your thoughts, feelings, behaviors, and the people you surround yourself with. Are your thoughts generally positive or negative? Do your behaviors align with your goals and values? Are your relationships supportive and uplifting?

Self-awareness is about recognizing patterns and understanding how they influence your life. It's about being mindful of your thoughts and how they affect your emotions, behaviors, and physical well-being. With this awareness, you can begin to make conscious choices that lead to positive changes.

Taking Control of Your Thoughts

The only person who can change your thoughts is you. While you can't always control the situations you find yourself in, you can control how you respond to them. This is the essence of CBT—recognizing that your thoughts influence your reality and that by changing your thoughts, you can change your life.

Start by identifying the negative thoughts that frequently come up for you. Write them down, and then challenge them. Are they based on facts, or are they assumptions? What evidence do you have to support or refute them? By critically examining your thoughts, you can begin to replace negative, unhelpful thoughts with more positive, realistic ones.

For example, if you often think, "I'm not good enough," challenge this thought by listing your accomplishments and strengths. Over time, this practice can help you shift your thought patterns and create a more positive CBT cycle.

The Power of Positivity

Positivity isn't just a feel-good concept; it's a powerful force that can transform your life. By focusing on positive thoughts, you can create a positive CBT cycle that leads to improved mental health, better relationships, and greater overall well-being.

58

The Energy of Positive Thoughts

Our thoughts carry energy that influences our emotions, behaviors, and the world around us. Positive thoughts generate positive energy, leading to feelings of happiness, contentment, and motivation. This, in turn, leads to positive behaviors, such as pursuing goals, building healthy relationships, and engaging in self-care.

For example, thinking, "I can handle this challenge" creates a sense of confidence and determination, leading to proactive behaviors like planning and problem-solving. This positive energy also influences those around you, creating a ripple effect of positivity.

The Maharishi Effect

One of the most compelling examples of the power of positive thinking and meditation is the Maharishi Effect. This phenomenon was observed when a large group of people meditated together, resulting in a significant decrease in crime and violence in the surrounding area. The Maharishi Effect demonstrates that collective positive energy can have a profound impact on the world.

This effect underscores the idea that our thoughts and energy are not isolated—they influence the world around us. By cultivating positive thoughts and energy, we can contribute to a more peaceful and harmonious world.

Imagine throwing a stone into a pond. The ripples spread out, affecting the entire surface of the water. Similarly, every thought, word, and action you have sends ripples into the world, influencing the people around you and the environment in which you live.

Creating Positive Ripples

Just as negativity can spread, so can positivity. By focusing on positive thoughts, speaking kind words, and engaging in positive actions, you can create ripples that spread positivity far beyond your immediate surroundings.

For example, offering a kind word to a stranger can brighten their day, and they may, in turn, pass that positivity on to someone else. This chain reaction can lead to a more positive and supportive community, one ripple at a time.

Harnessing Your Inner Power for Positive Change

Recognizing the power of your thoughts and actions is the first step in harnessing your inner power for positive change. By focusing on positivity and making conscious choices, you can create a life filled with joy, purpose, and fulfilment.

Breaking Negative Cycles

Negative thought patterns can be deeply ingrained, often passed down through generations. These patterns, rooted in past trauma or learned behaviors, can keep individuals stuck in cycles of negativity. Breaking these cycles is essential for creating a healthier and more fulfilling life.

Understanding Generational Trauma

Generational trauma refers to the transmission of trauma across generations. This can be the result of historical events like wars, systemic oppression, or family dynamics. The effects of trauma can influence thoughts, behaviors, and even genetic expression, leading to patterns of negativity that persist across generations.

For example, a family that has experienced poverty for generations might pass down a mindset of scarcity, leading to thoughts like "There will never be enough." This mindset could shape how family members view the world, make decisions or react in certain situations, often leading to anxiety, mistrust or fear of taking risks. This negative thinking can become deeply ingrained, affecting the way future generations think, feel and behave, even if they have not directly experienced the original trauma. Breaking these patterns require awareness, understanding and often professional support so that future generations can build healthier mindsets and behaviors.

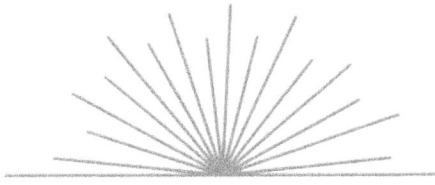

Chapter 8

Reclaiming Your Power: The Art of Not Being Easily Offended

Being offended by others' actions can block our ability to focus on what truly matters to us, diverting our energy and attention away from our goals. When we allow ourselves to be affected by the words or behaviors of others, our thoughts become entangled in negativity, leading to a chain reaction of negative experiences and interactions. This reactive state not only drains our mental and emotional resources but also clouds our judgment, preventing us from manifesting the life we desire. However, when we master the art of not being affected by others, we reclaim our power. By choosing to remain centered and unbothered, we free ourselves from the influence of external forces, allowing us to focus on our true desires and create a life aligned with our highest potential.

In a world where people's actions and words are often sharp, unkind, or simply thoughtless, it's easy to feel offended. A rude comment, a dismissive attitude, or an inconsiderate action can leave us feeling hurt, angry, and disrespected. But what if the key to inner peace and emotional freedom lies not in trying to change how others treat us, but in changing how we respond to it? This chapter is about stepping into a mindset where we stop being easily offended, where we no longer give our power away to the opinions and actions of others, and where we learn to let go of the ego that demands validation and recognition.

Understanding the Ego: The Root of Offense

At the heart of most offenses lies the ego—the part of us that craves acknowledgment, validation, and respect. The ego is deeply concerned with how others perceive us, constantly seeking approval and fearing rejection. When someone is rude or dismissive, the ego interprets this as a personal attack, triggering feelings of anger, insecurity, or indignation. The ego takes everything personally, making it easy to get offended even when the slight is minor or unintentional.

But here's a truth that's worth remembering: when someone is rude or unkind, it's not really about you; it's about them. People's behavior is a reflection of their own inner world—what they think, feel, and believe. If someone lashes out, belittles you, or dismisses you, it often stems from their own insecurities, frustrations, or unresolved issues. They project their negativity outward because they haven't learned how to manage it internally.

When we understand this, we can begin to detach from taking others' behavior so personally. Their words and actions are their responsibility, not ours. By recognizing that their rudeness or disrespect is more about their internal struggle than it is about our worth, we can step back and reclaim our peace.

Letting Go of the Need for Validation

One of the reasons we get easily offended is because we subconsciously seek validation from others. We want to be liked, respected, and valued. When someone acts in a way that suggests they don't see our worth, it can feel like a personal attack. But here's the paradox: the more we depend on external validation, the more fragile our sense of self becomes.

When we let go of the need for others to validate us, we become more resilient. We stop hinging our self-worth on how others treat us, and we start relying on our own inner confidence. We become grounded in knowing who we are, what we value, and what we bring to the world. When this internal foundation is strong, it's much harder for others to shake us. Their opinions and behaviors lose their power to hurt us because we no longer need their approval to feel whole.

This doesn't mean we become indifferent or apathetic; it simply means we stop giving people the power to control our emotions. We can acknowledge their actions without internalizing them. We can recognize someone's rudeness or judgment without letting it define how we feel about ourselves. In this way, we protect our peace and maintain control over our emotional state.

Don't Give Away Your Power

Every time we get offended by someone's words or actions; we give away a bit of our power. We allow them to dictate how we feel, letting their behavior determine our mood and emotions. When we're easily offended, we're in a constant state of reaction—our happiness and peace of mind become dependent on how others treat us. This is a vulnerable way to live because it puts our well-being in the hands of other people, many of whom we can't control.

By choosing not to take offense, we take our power back. We become the ones in charge of our emotional state, deciding how we want to feel regardless of what's happening around us. This doesn't mean we ignore our emotions or pretend that hurtful things don't affect us; it means we process those emotions in a healthy way without letting them control us. We acknowledge the pain, but we don't dwell on it or let it fester. We feel it, learn from it, and then let it go.

Processing and Letting Go: The Power of Forgiveness

When someone does something hurtful, it's natural to feel upset, angry, or betrayed. But holding onto those emotions can quickly turn into bitterness and resentment, which only harms us in the long run. Forgiveness is often misunderstood as letting someone "off the hook" or condoning their behavior, but that's not what it's really about. Forgiveness is about freeing ourselves from the negative energy that comes from holding onto grudges. It's about choosing not to let someone's actions continue to have power over us.

When we refuse to forgive, we keep ourselves locked in a cycle of negativity. The anger and resentment we hold onto affect our mood, our thoughts, and ultimately, our quality of life. By forgiving, we release that toxic energy and allow ourselves to move on. This doesn't mean we have to forget what happened or allow someone to mistreat us again; it simply means we stop letting their actions dictate our emotions and our mindset.

Forgiveness is an act of self-care. It's a way of saying, "I choose peace over anger. I choose freedom over holding onto pain." When we let go of the need to be right, the need for an apology, or the need for others to see things our way, we find a deeper sense of peace. We stop being controlled by what others do and start living according to our own values and principles.

Know Yourself and Stand Firm in Your Truth

One of the most powerful ways to avoid being easily offended is to truly know yourself. When you have a clear sense of who you are, what you stand for, and what you value, other people's opinions or judgments lose their power over you. You become grounded in your own truth, and that foundation becomes unshakeable.

People will always have opinions, and some of those opinions may be negative. But their thoughts are just that—their thoughts. They don't define you unless you allow them to. When you know yourself deeply, you become less concerned with what others think. You no longer seek external validation because you are secure in your own self-worth.

This inner security allows you to navigate the world with confidence and grace. When someone is rude, dismissive, or judgmental, you don't feel the need to defend yourself or prove them wrong. You can simply acknowledge their behavior for what it is—a reflection of them, not you—and move on with your peace intact.

Conclusion: Choosing Freedom over Offense

In life, we will inevitably encounter people who are rude, judgmental, or unkind. But how we choose to respond is entirely within our control. By letting go of the need for validation, processing our emotions in a healthy way, and standing firm in our own truth, we can stop being easily offended. We can reclaim our power and live with greater peace, resilience, and inner freedom.

Remember, the world is full of people projecting their own insecurities and unresolved issues. Their behavior is about them, not you. By letting go of the ego's need to take everything personally, we can rise above the pettiness, keep our peace, and live with a deeper sense of purpose and joy. Don't give away your power—choose to be unbothered, grounded, and free.

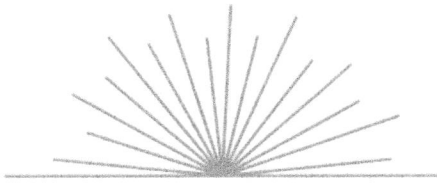

Chapter 9

Disconnection and the Virtual Life

Introduction: The Modern Disconnect

In the rapidly advancing digital age, humanity has grown increasingly distanced from its roots and its essence. The natural world, once a central part of daily life, is now something many experience only occasionally, if at all. The omnipresence of technology—smartphones, social media, streaming services, and constant connectivity—has created a virtual bubble that cocoons us from the real world. This chapter explores the consequences of this disconnection, particularly how it influences our sense of self, our relationships, and our mental health. It also highlights how the distractions of living in a virtual world is blocking us from going after all of our dreams and desires.

The Modern World: A Life Enveloped in Screens

As you walk down the street, it's common to see people engrossed in their phones, oblivious to their surroundings. Whether it's texting, checking social media, or streaming videos, the screen often takes precedence over real-life interactions and the environment. This constant engagement with technology has profound effects on how we perceive the world and ourselves.

The digital world, while offering endless information and entertainment, also leads to a sensory overload that diminishes our capacity to appreciate the simpler, more grounding aspects of life. The warmth of the sun, the rustle of leaves in the wind, the laughter of a friend—these are often missed in favor of notifications and virtual interactions. This disconnection from the natural world and the present moment can lead to a sense of emptiness, as if something essential is missing from our lives.

Social Media: The Illusion of Connection

Social media was created to bring people closer, to connect friends and family across distances, and to foster new relationships. However, it often does the opposite. Platforms like Instagram, Facebook, and TikTok offer curated glimpses into others' lives—pictures of perfect vacations, idealized relationships, and flawless appearances. This constant exposure to the seemingly perfect lives of others can create feelings of inadequacy, jealousy, and depression.

Many young people, in particular, struggle with this phenomenon. They compare their lives to the highlights of others, not realizing that what they see online is a filtered version of reality. This can lead to a distorted self-image and a belief that their own lives are lacking. The rise in mental health issues among adolescents in recent years correlates with the increased use of social media, highlighting the potential dangers of these platforms.

The Statistics: A Worrying Trend

The numbers paint a stark picture. Between 2009 and 2017, the rate of depression among adolescents increased by 63%, while reports of suicidal thoughts rose by 43%. For young girls, the situation is even more alarming, with self-harm incidents nearly tripling. These statistics are more than just numbers; they represent real lives affected by the pressures and influences of the virtual world. The impact of social media on mental health is significant and cannot be ignored.

The Social Dilemma: A Glimpse Behind the Curtain

The documentary "The Social Dilemma" offers an insider's perspective on the inner workings of social media platforms. Featuring interviews with former employees of major tech companies, the film reveals how these platforms are designed to be addictive, using algorithms to keep users engaged for as long as possible. These companies collect vast amounts of data on their users, which they then use to create personalized content and advertisements, further entrenching users in the virtual world.

What's particularly revealing is that many of these tech insiders' express concerns about the platforms they helped create. They acknowledge the negative impact on mental health and admit that they ban or limit their own children's use of these platforms. This insight underscores the manipulative nature of social media, where users are not the customers but the product. The data generated by users is sold to advertisers, creating a system where profit is prioritized over well-being.

Mainstream Media and the Perpetuation of Stress

It's not just social media that contributes to our modern disconnection—mainstream media plays a significant role as well. News outlets, driven by the need to attract viewers and readers, often focus on negative stories. Violence, disaster, and scandal dominate headlines, creating a skewed perception of the world. This constant exposure to negativity can lead to increased anxiety and stress, as people begin to believe that the world is more dangerous and chaotic than it actually is.

Moreover, media bias further complicates this issue. News is often presented from a specific political, cultural, or religious perspective, influencing how events are perceived. This can result in a one-sided understanding of complex issues, reinforcing pre-existing beliefs and contributing to societal division.

The Power of the Media: Shaping Public Perception

The media's influence on public opinion cannot be overstated. As Malcolm X famously said, "The media is the most powerful entity on Earth. They have the power to make the innocent guilty and to make the guilty innocent, and that's power. Because they control the minds of the masses." This statement highlights the need for critical thinking when consuming media. It is essential to question the information presented to us, seek out diverse perspectives, and engage in independent research to form our own opinions.

Stress as a Health Crisis: The Hidden Epidemic

Chronic stress is a significant health issue in modern society. It is linked to 97% of diseases, including heart disease, diabetes, and mental health disorders. The pressures of modern life—work, social expectations, and the relentless pace of technology—contribute to this epidemic. Many people feel overwhelmed by the demands placed on them, leading to burnout, anxiety, and a host of physical ailments.

The constant connectivity that technology offers can exacerbate stress. The expectation to be always available, to respond to messages and emails immediately, and to keep up with the latest news and trends can leave little time for relaxation and self-care. This relentless pace can lead to exhaustion and a sense of never being able to keep up.

Work and Society Pressures: The Cost of Overwork

In many cultures, particularly in the West, there is a glorification of overwork. Long hours and constant busyness are often seen as signs of success and dedication. However, this work culture can have severe consequences for both mental and physical health. Burnout, characterized by emotional exhaustion, detachment, and a sense of ineffectiveness, is becoming increasingly common. The pressure to perform and achieve can lead to chronic stress, which in turn can lead to serious health issues.

The education system is another source of stress, particularly for students and teachers. The focus on standardized testing and performance metrics creates a high-pressure environment where the holistic development of students is often overlooked. This can lead to anxiety, depression, and a lack of engagement in learning. Teachers, too, are affected by the increasing demands of paperwork, administrative tasks, and the pressure to meet performance targets, leading to burnout and high turnover rates.

The Future Generation: The Impact on Children

Children today face numerous challenges that previous generations could not have imagined. From early exposure to technology to the pressures of an increasingly competitive education system, the environment in which they are growing up is vastly different from that of their parents. The decline in social skills, language development, and behavior in young children is a concerning trend. Reduced parental interaction, increased screen time, and the pressures of modern life all contribute to these issues.

Early childhood is a critical period for development, and the experiences and environment during these years can have long-lasting effects. The Royal Foundation's research on early years highlights the importance of addressing the root causes of social challenges, such as poor mental health and family breakdown, through early intervention. The education system, too, needs reform to prioritize the well-being and holistic development of children. Reducing the focus on standardized testing and increasing support for children with special needs are essential steps towards creating a supportive and nurturing environment in schools.

Conclusion: Reconnecting with Ourselves and the World

The issues of modern distractions, media influence, stress, and the challenges faced by the younger generation are complex and multifaceted. However, addressing them is crucial for creating a healthier and more balanced society. It starts with fostering a deeper connection with our true selves and the world around us. This means stepping away from screens, engaging with nature, and being present in our interactions with others.

Critical thinking and media literacy are also essential in navigating the information overload of the digital age. By questioning the information presented to us and seeking out diverse perspectives, we can form a more balanced and informed view of the world.

Finally, creating supportive environments—both at home and in schools—is key to ensuring the healthy development of future generations. By prioritizing well-being over performance, we can help children develop the skills and resilience they need to thrive in an increasingly complex world.

This chapter has explored the ways in which modern life can lead to disconnection, stress, and mental health challenges. In the following chapters, we will delve deeper into these themes, exploring strategies for reconnecting with our true selves, managing stress, and creating a more fulfilling and balanced life.

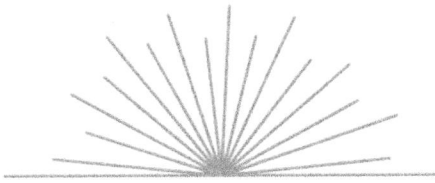

Chapter 10

The Magnetic Power of Thoughts and the Expansive Energy of Focus

Introduction

The idea that our thoughts are magnetic and that our energy acts as a currency is at the core of many spiritual and philosophical teachings. This concept suggests that whatever we focus on—whether positive or negative—will expand and manifest in our lives. Our thoughts, like magnets, attract experiences, people, and circumstances that resonate with the energy we project. Similarly, where we invest our emotional and mental energy determines what grows and thrives in our lives.

In this chapter, we will explore how your thoughts act as magnets that draw into your life the very things you dwell on, and how the energy you spend on certain thoughts or feelings will cause them to expand. We will delve into practical examples to illustrate these principles and demonstrate how focusing on lack or what you don't have can inadvertently attract more of the same, while focusing on abundance and gratitude can bring forth prosperity and joy.

The Magnetic Power of Thoughts

At the heart of the belief that thoughts are magnetic is the understanding that the mind and the universe are deeply interconnected. Just as a magnet attracts objects within its field, your thoughts attract experiences and outcomes that align with their frequency. When you focus on something consistently, you send out a signal, a vibrational frequency, that resonates with similar energies in the universe.

Thoughts as Energetic Vibrations: Thoughts are not just abstract concepts; they are energetic vibrations that interact with the universe. Every thought carries a certain frequency, and this frequency has the power to attract similar frequencies. When you dwell on a particular thought or idea, you strengthen its vibrational energy, making it more likely to manifest in your life.

Consider someone who frequently worries about their health. The constant worry sends out a vibration of fear and anxiety, which can attract experiences that validate those fears, such as illness or stress. Conversely, a person who focuses on thoughts of health and well-being sends out a vibration of vitality, attracting circumstances that support their physical and mental health.

The Subconscious Mind: The subconscious mind plays a crucial role in this process. It does not distinguish between what is real and what is imagined; it simply acts on the thoughts and images that are repeatedly impressed upon it. When you consistently focus on a particular thought, the subconscious mind accepts it as a truth and begins to shape your reality to match it.

For example, if you repeatedly tell yourself that you are unlucky in love, your subconscious mind will internalize this belief, leading you to act in ways that sabotage potential relationships. On the other hand, if you affirm that you are deserving of love and happiness, your subconscious mind will guide you toward actions and behaviors that attract healthy, loving relationships.

74

Energy as a Currency

The concept that energy is a currency suggests that where you direct your focus, attention, and emotional energy will determine what grows and flourishes in your life. Just as financial investments grow over time, the thoughts and feelings you "spend" your energy on will expand and multiply.

1. The Investment of Attention: Your attention is one of your most powerful resources. Whatever you focus on, you give energy to, and whatever you give energy to will expand. This is true for both positive and negative thoughts.

For example, if you spend your energy worrying about your job, you might find that your work situation becomes increasingly stressful. By focusing on the negatives, you give them more power, allowing them to dominate your experience. On the other hand, if you focus your energy on aspects of your job that you enjoy or on the opportunities it provides, you might find that your work experience improves, attracting more positive situations and outcomes.

2. Energy and Emotional States: Emotions are a form of energy that can either uplift or deplete you. When you dwell on negative emotions like fear, anger, or jealousy, you invest your energy in those feelings, and as a result, they grow stronger. This can lead to a downward spiral where negative emotions feed on themselves, attracting more negativity into your life.

Conversely, when you focus on positive emotions like gratitude, love, and joy, you invest your energy in these uplifting states, causing them to expand. This creates a positive feedback loop where good feelings attract more good experiences, leading to a more fulfilling and joyful life.

3. The Expansion Principle: The principle of expansion states that whatever you give your energy to, will grow. This means that if you focus on problems, challenges, or what you lack, you will attract more of the same. But if you focus on solutions, opportunities, and abundance, these positive aspects of life will expand.

For example, someone who constantly complains about not having enough money will likely continue to experience financial scarcity. Their focus on lack reinforces the experience of lack. However, if that person shifts their focus to the money they do have, expressing gratitude for it, and visualizing financial abundance, they may begin to attract more wealth and financial opportunities.

Examples of Focus and Expansion

To better understand these principles, let's explore some examples that illustrate how thoughts and energy work as magnets and currency.

1. Focusing on Lack: Imagine a person who constantly worries about not having enough money. They check their bank account obsessively, stress over every bill, and frequently talk about their financial difficulties. Their thoughts are consumed with fear and anxiety about money, and their energy is spent reinforcing the idea of scarcity.

As a result, this person continues to experience financial hardship. Their focus on lack attracts more situations that confirm their fears—unexpected expenses, job instability, and missed opportunities. Their energy, spent on worrying about what they don't have, only serves to expand the experience of lack in their life.

Now, contrast this with someone who, despite having limited resources, focuses on gratitude for what they do have. They may not be wealthy, but they choose to focus on the small financial victories—paying off a debt, finding a great deal, or receiving unexpected income. This person spends their energy on appreciating abundance, even in small amounts. Over time, they begin to attract more opportunities for financial growth, such as a new job offer, a profitable investment, or a gift of money. Their focus on abundance expands their experience of it.

2. Health and Well-being: Consider an individual who is constantly concerned about their health. They frequently think about getting sick, imagine worst-case scenarios, and dwell on every minor symptom. This focus on illness creates a vibration of fear and anxiety, which can weaken the immune system and actually increase the likelihood of becoming ill. Their energy is spent worrying about potential health problems, which causes these concerns to expand.

On the other hand, another person might choose to focus on thoughts of health, vitality, and well-being. They imagine themselves feeling strong, energetic, and healthy. They invest their energy in activities that support their health, such as exercise, eating nutritious foods, and practicing mindfulness. This focus on health and positive energy attracts more experiences of well-being, such as faster recovery from illness, greater physical stamina, and an overall sense of vitality. Their energy, spent on thoughts of health, causes health to expand in their life.

3. Relationships: In relationships, the magnetic power of thoughts and the currency of energy are especially evident. Imagine someone who constantly fears being abandoned or unloved. They focus on past hurts, worry about being rejected, and interpret neutral situations as signs of impending doom. This focus on fear and rejection attracts experiences that mirror these feelings—arguments, misunderstandings, and emotional distance. The energy spent on fearing abandonment causes that fear to expand, often leading to the very outcome they dread.

Conversely, consider someone who focuses on love, trust, and connection in their relationships. They choose to see the best in their partner, express gratitude for the love they share, and invest their energy in nurturing the relationship. This positive focus attracts more love and understanding, leading to deeper intimacy and a stronger bond. The energy spent on cultivating love causes love to expand in their relationship.

Shifting Focus from Lack to Abundance

Understanding the magnetic power of thoughts and the expansive nature of energy is the first step in consciously shaping your reality. The next step is learning how to shift your focus from lack to abundance, from fear to love, and from problems to solutions.

1. Mindful Awareness: The first step in shifting your focus is becoming aware of where your thoughts and energy are currently directed. Pay attention to your habitual thought patterns, especially those that

involve worry, fear, or lack. Notice how these thoughts make you feel and how they influence your actions and experiences.

For example, if you find yourself constantly worrying about money, recognize this pattern and the feelings it generates. Awareness is the key to change; once you are aware of your negative focus, you can begin to redirect it.

2. Gratitude Practice: One of the most effective ways to shift your focus from lack to abundance is through the practice of gratitude. Gratitude shifts your attention away from what you don't have and towards what you do have, creating a vibration of abundance and positivity.

Start by making a daily habit of writing down things you are grateful for, no matter how small. This could be as simple as appreciating a sunny day, a good meal, or a warm smile from a stranger. By consistently acknowledging the positive aspects of your life, you cultivate a mindset that attracts more of what you appreciate, ultimately leading to a greater sense of fulfilment and abundance.

A Tale of Two Mornings: The Power of Perspective

The Negative Start: Thomas's Morning

Thomas's alarm buzzed at 6:30 AM, jarring him out of a restless sleep. As soon as his eyes opened, a wave of dread washed over him. The day ahead felt like a mountain he had no energy to climb. "Ugh, another day of the same old crap," he muttered to himself as he dragged himself out of bed. His thoughts immediately spiraled into negativity: the pile of work waiting for him, the stressful meeting he had later, and the constant feeling that life was passing him by without much improvement.

As he prepared for the day, his focus was on everything that could go wrong. His mind zeroed in on the blemish on his face that had appeared overnight. "Of course," he thought bitterly, "just one more thing to deal with." He burned his toast, tripped over the dog's bowl, and stubbed his toe on the way to the bathroom. "Great, just great," he muttered, feeling his frustration grow.

On his way to work, Thomas noticed every inconvenience: the heavy traffic, the rude driver who cut him off, the long line at the coffee shop. His mind, wired by his Reticular Activating System (RAS), was tuned in to negativity. The RAS is a network of neurons in the brain that acts like a filter, determining what we notice and focus on. Thomas's negative mood and thoughts activated his RAS to filter for negative experiences, confirming his belief that the day was going to be awful.

At work, Thomas's mindset attracted more negativity. He interpreted his boss's neutral feedback as criticism, felt slighted when a colleague didn't greet him, and struggled to concentrate during his meeting, assuming that his ideas weren't good enough. By lunchtime, Thomas was exhausted and his mood had plummeted even further. His RAS had reinforced his negative outlook, filtering out any positive experiences or opportunities for joy.

The Positive Start: Lucas's Morning

Across town, Lucas's alarm also buzzed at 6:30 AM, but he greeted the day with a different mindset. He took a deep breath and stretched, feeling grateful for the chance to start fresh. "Today is going to be a good day," he said to himself, smiling as he rolled out of bed. Lucas had trained himself to focus on the positives, no matter how small they might seem. He knew that how he started his day would set the tone for everything that followed.

As Lucas got ready, he noticed the golden sunlight streaming through the window, filling his room with warmth. "What a beautiful morning," he thought, savoring the moment. When he accidentally spilled his coffee, he simply chuckled and thought, "No big deal, I'll make another." His mind was set to find the good in every situation.

On his commute, Lucas's RAS filtered the world differently. He noticed the flowers blooming along the roadside, the kindness of the barista who remembered his order, and the catchy tune on the radio that lifted his spirits. He felt a sense of calm as he navigated through traffic, grateful for the extra time to listen to his favorite podcast. His positive outlook was further reinforced by his RAS, which highlighted the good and minimized the bad.

At work, Lucas's day unfolded in alignment with his optimistic start. He approached his tasks with enthusiasm and saw challenges as opportunities to grow. When his boss gave him feedback, he saw it as constructive and a chance to improve. He greeted his colleagues with a smile, and they responded in kind. Even when small hiccups occurred, Lucas's positive mindset and the filtering mechanism of his RAS helped him to stay focused on solutions rather than problems.

The Science Behind the Stories: The RAS at Work

The contrasting experiences of Thomas and Lucas illustrate the powerful role of the Reticular Activating System (RAS) in shaping our perception of reality. The RAS is like the brain's gatekeeper, filtering out the vast amount of information we encounter and letting through only what aligns with our current focus and beliefs. In Thomas's case, his negative thoughts set his RAS to filter for negativity, leading him to notice and attract more negative experiences throughout his day. His brain was wired to seek out and confirm his pessimistic outlook, which created a self-fulfilling prophecy of misery.

On the other hand, Lucas's positive mindset activated his RAS to filter for positivity, allowing him to notice and amplify the good in his day. His brain was trained to focus on uplifting experiences and opportunities, leading to a more fulfilling and joyful day. The RAS didn't change the external circumstances— both men faced similar challenges—but it dramatically influenced how each perceived and responded to those circumstances.

The Choice is Yours

Thomas and Lucas's stories highlight an essential truth: our thoughts and attitudes are powerful tools that shape our reality. The RAS in our brain doesn't judge whether our focus is positive or negative—it simply amplifies what we choose to concentrate on. By becoming aware of this, we can take control of our thought patterns and consciously direct our RAS to filter for positivity, joy, and success.

The choice is yours each morning. Will you let negativity dominate and let your RAS confirm it, or will you choose a positive mindset and let your brain filter the world to support your happiness and goals?

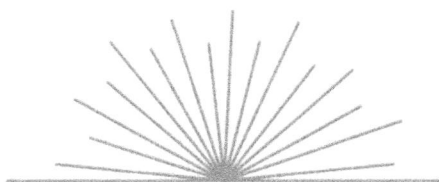

Chapter 11

Stepping Into Your Power: Embracing Energy, Focus, and Boundaries

Understanding Your Power: Energy and Focus

Stepping into your power is about embracing your inherent energy and focus. This power is not about control over others or external circumstances but about mastering your own inner world. Your power is your energy—the vital force that drives your actions, decisions, and overall state of being. It is also your focus—the ability to direct your attention toward what truly matters, while filtering out distractions and negativity.

As previously discussed, when you let someone else dictate how you feel or react, you surrender your power. This happens when we internalize unkind words, allow circumstances to disrupt our peace, or react impulsively to challenges. These reactions drain our energy and scatter our focus, leaving us feeling depleted and disempowered. However, by recognizing that your power lies within you, in how you choose to respond to life, you can begin to reclaim it.

The Impact of Reacting to Negativity

Every time we react negatively to someone or something, we inadvertently give away a piece of our power. When someone is unkind or circumstances turn unfavorable, it is natural to feel a surge of emotions—anger, frustration, sadness, or even fear. These emotions are valid, and it's important to acknowledge them. However, how we choose to express and process these emotions is crucial. Reacting impulsively, whether through words or actions, often leads to regret and further disempowerment. It's in these moments that we hand over control of our energy to external forces, allowing them to dictate our state of mind and overall well-being.

For example, imagine you're in a meeting at work and a colleague makes a snide remark about your recent project. Your initial reaction might be anger or hurt, and you may feel the urge to snap back or defend yourself aggressively. While this might provide momentary relief, it often leads to unnecessary conflict and diminishes your professional demeanor. In this scenario, your power is handed over to the colleague, as they have successfully disrupted your focus and emotional equilibrium.

Instead, by pausing and taking a deep breath, you create space to choose your response deliberately. You might decide to calmly address the comment later, in private, or let it go if it doesn't warrant a response. By doing so, you maintain control over your energy and focus, preserving your power and demonstrating emotional intelligence.

The Role of Boundaries in Protecting Your Power

To minimize encounters with people and circumstances that are not aligned with your values and well-being, it is essential to set clear boundaries. Boundaries are the guidelines you establish to protect your energy, focus, and overall sense of self. They help you define what is acceptable and unacceptable in your interactions with others and in your engagement with the world.

Setting boundaries is not about building walls or isolating yourself from others. Instead, it is about creating a safe space where you can thrive and maintain your power. Boundaries help you manage your energy more effectively by preventing it from being drained by toxic people, situations, or habits. They also help you stay focused on your goals and values, ensuring that you do not get sidetracked by distractions or negative influences.

How to Set Boundaries: Practical Steps

1. **Identify Your Needs and Values** The first step in setting boundaries is to identify what matters most to you. What are your core values? What do you need to feel safe, respected, and fulfilled? Understanding your needs and values is crucial because it provides the foundation for your boundaries. For example, if you value honesty, you may need to set boundaries with people who tend to be deceitful or manipulative.

Take time to reflect on past experiences where you felt your energy was drained or your focus was disrupted. What triggered those feelings? Was it a person, a situation, or perhaps your own lack of clarity about your boundaries? By understanding these triggers, you can start to recognize patterns and identify where boundaries are needed.

2. **Communicate Your Boundaries Clearly** Once you've identified your boundaries, the next step is to communicate them clearly and assertively. This means expressing your needs and limits in a way that is respectful but firm. Remember, your boundaries are not up for negotiation—they are non-negotiable aspects of your well-being.

For example, if you have a friend who frequently cancels plans at the last minute, leaving you feeling disrespected, you might say, "I value our time together, but when plans are cancelled last minute, it feels like my time isn't respected. I'd appreciate it if we could confirm our plans ahead of time or reschedule with more notice." This approach is direct yet considerate, conveying your boundary without causing unnecessary conflict.

It's important to be consistent in communicating your boundaries. If you set a boundary and then repeatedly allow it to be crossed, it sends a message that your boundaries are not serious. This can lead to confusion and further violations of your limits. Stand firm in your boundaries, and others will learn to respect them.

3. **Learn to Say No** Saying no is one of the most powerful ways to protect your energy and focus. It's a simple word, yet many of us struggle with it, often out of fear of disappointing others or being perceived as difficult. However, saying yes to everything often leads to overwhelm, resentment, and a loss of personal power.

To step into your power, you must become comfortable with saying no when something does not align with your values, needs, or goals. This doesn't mean you have to be harsh or unkind—no can be expressed in a compassionate and respectful manner. For instance, if you're asked to take on an additional project at work that would stretch your capacity, you might say, "I appreciate the opportunity, but I'm currently focused on other priorities and won't be able to commit fully to this project."

Saying no is not just about declining requests from others—it's also about saying no to your own tendencies to overextend yourself, engage in negative self-talk, or indulge in habits that drain your energy. By setting limits on these behaviors, you reclaim your power and create more space for what truly matters.

4. **Enforce Your Boundaries** Setting and communicating boundaries is only effective if you also enforce them. This means taking action when a boundary is crossed and holding others accountable for their actions. Enforcement doesn't have to be confrontational, but it does require firmness and consistency.

For example, if you've set a boundary that you will not engage in work-related discussions after 7 PM, but a colleague repeatedly calls you during that time, you need to reinforce your boundary. You might remind them of your boundary and let them know that you will only respond during work hours. If the behavior continues, you may need to escalate your response, such as by not answering calls after hours or addressing the issue with your manager.

Enforcing boundaries also means being prepared to walk away from situations or relationships that consistently violate your limits. This can be challenging, especially if the person or situation is important to you. However, protecting your energy and focus is paramount, and sometimes this means making difficult decisions to preserve your well-being.

5. **Practice Self-Care** is a crucial aspect of maintaining your boundaries and staying in your power. When you prioritize self-care, you reinforce the message that your well-being is important and non-negotiable. Self-care practices can range from physical activities, like exercise and proper nutrition, to mental and emotional activities, such as meditation, journaling, or spending time in nature.

Regular self-care replenishes your energy and strengthens your resolve to maintain your boundaries. It also helps you stay grounded and focused, making it easier to navigate challenges and resist the temptation to give away your power. Remember, self-care is not a luxury—it is a necessity for sustaining your energy and staying aligned with your values.

The Power of Letting Go

Another key aspect of stepping into your power is learning to let go of what no longer serves you. This includes letting go of toxic relationships, outdated beliefs, and unnecessary commitments. Holding on to these things can drain your energy and scatter your focus, leaving you feeling stuck and disempowered.

Letting go is not always easy—it often involves facing discomfort and uncertainty. However, by releasing what no longer serves you, you create space for new opportunities, relationships, and experiences that are more aligned with your values and goals. This act of letting go is a powerful reclaiming of your energy and focus, allowing you to step more fully into your power.

Embracing Your Authentic Self

Stepping into your power also means embracing your authentic self—your true thoughts, feelings, and desires, free from external expectations or societal pressures. When you align with your authentic self, you operate from a place of truth and integrity, which naturally strengthens your energy and focus.

To embrace your authentic self, it's important to practice self-awareness and self-acceptance. This means regularly checking in with yourself to ensure that your actions and decisions are in line with your true values and desires. It also means accepting yourself as you are, with all your strengths and imperfections, and resisting the urge to conform to others' expectations.

When you operate from your authentic self, you become more resilient to external influences and better able to protect your power. You no longer feel the need to seek validation or approval from others, because you are grounded in your own truth. This self-alignment is one of the most empowering states you can achieve, as it allows you to navigate life with confidence, clarity, and purpose.

Conclusion: Living in Your Power

Stepping into your power is a lifelong journey of self-discovery, growth, and empowerment. It involves recognizing that your power lies within you, in how you choose to manage your energy and focus. By setting clear boundaries, learning to say no, and embracing your authentic self, you can protect your power and live a life that is aligned with your true values and desires.

Remember, your power is not about controlling others or external circumstances—it's about mastering your inner world and responding to life with intention and grace. As you continue to step into your power, you will find that you are more resilient, focused, and fulfilled, capable of navigating life's challenges with ease and confidence.

In this empowered state, you become the creator of your reality, shaping your life according to your own values and desires. You no longer allow others to determine who and what you should be or feel, because you are firmly rooted in your own power. This is the ultimate expression of personal freedom and the key to living a life of purpose, abundance, and joy.

THE POWER OF YOU

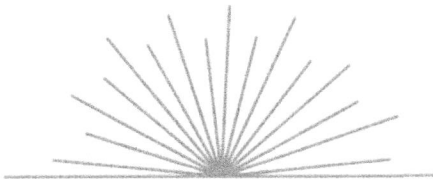

Chapter 12

Our Circumstances Don't Define You: The Power of Belief in Creating Your Reality

Understanding the Power of Belief

We often hear stories of people who have seemingly defied the odds to achieve extraordinary success. Whether it's earning a seven-figure income with what appears to be minimal effort, building a thriving business from the ground up, or living a life filled with joy and fulfilment despite humble beginnings, these individuals share one thing in common: an unshakeable belief in their own potential. It's easy to look at these stories and think, "That could never be me." But the truth is, the only thing standing between you and the life you desire is your belief system.

Your circumstances—the external conditions of your life—don't define who you are or what you're capable of achieving. What defines you is how you perceive and respond to those circumstances. The beliefs you hold about yourself, your abilities, and the world around you play a crucial role in shaping your reality. If someone else can earn seven figures doing relatively little, so can you. The difference lies in your belief system, and by working on it, you can begin to unlock your full potential.

The Myth of Circumstances as Limitations

From a young age, many of us are conditioned to believe that our circumstances—our family background, education, financial situation, or even our physical environment—determine our destiny. We're taught that if we're born into poverty, it's difficult to escape it; if we don't have a college degree, our career options are limited; or if we live in a certain neighborhood, our opportunities for success are constrained. While it's true that circumstances can influence our experiences, they do not have the final say in our lives.

Circumstances are temporary and can change. They are not permanent fixtures that lock us into a certain path. The key to breaking free from the limitations of our circumstances lies in understanding that they are not the ultimate determinant of our success. Instead, it's our beliefs about what is possible that shape our reality. If you believe that your circumstances are holding you back, then they will. But if you believe that you have the power to change your circumstances and create the life you desire, then that belief will become your reality.

The key takeaway here is that it's not the circumstances themselves that dictate your success, but your beliefs about those circumstances. If you believe that you are capable of earning seven figures, then you will take the necessary steps to make that a reality. If you believe that you are stuck in a certain situation, then you will continue to live within the confines of that belief.

The Role of Self-Image in Success

Your self-image—the way you see yourself—plays a critical role in determining your success. If you see yourself as capable, deserving, and successful, you are more likely to take the actions necessary to achieve your goals. However, if your self-image is tied to your current circumstances or past experiences, it can limit your ability to see beyond those limitations.

To change your self-image, start by visualizing yourself as the person you want to become. Picture yourself living the life you desire, with all the success, abundance, and fulfilment that comes with it. See yourself as confident, empowered, and capable of achieving anything you set your mind to.

Visualization is a powerful tool because it helps to reprogram your subconscious mind. When you consistently visualize yourself as successful, your mind begins to accept this new self-image as reality, and you start to act in ways that align with that image.

Success Stories: Proof That Belief Transcends Circumstances

There are countless stories of individuals who have overcome seemingly insurmountable odds to achieve incredible success. These stories serve as powerful reminders that our circumstances do not define us; our beliefs do.

Take, for example, Oprah Winfrey, who was born into poverty and faced numerous challenges throughout her early life, including abuse and discrimination. Despite these circumstances, she believed in her potential and pursued her dreams relentlessly. Today, she is one of the most successful and influential women in the world, with a net worth of billions.

Or consider the story of J.K. Rowling, who wrote the first Harry Potter book while living on welfare as a single mother. At the time, Rowling was struggling with depression, financial hardship, and the responsibility of raising her daughter alone. Despite her difficult circumstances, she believed in the story she was writing and her ability to make a difference with her work. She persisted, and after numerous rejections from publishers, the Harry Potter series was eventually accepted and went on to become one of the best-selling book series in history, making Rowling one of the wealthiest and most influential authors in the world.

These examples, and countless others like them, illustrate a fundamental truth: your circumstances do not determine your destiny—your belief system does. Both Oprah and J.K. Rowling could have easily allowed their challenging circumstances to define them, to accept the notion that success was out of reach. Instead, they chose to believe in their potential and to act on that belief, despite the obstacles in their path.

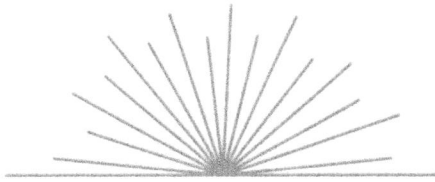

Chapter 13

The Power of Beliefs: How to Identify and Overcome Limiting Beliefs

The Role of Beliefs in Shaping Our Reality

Our lives are shaped by what we assume and believe. These beliefs act as a lens through which we perceive and interact with the world, influencing our thoughts, emotions, and actions. Whether we are aware of it or not, our beliefs dictate the opportunities we see, the choices we make, and the results we achieve. They form the foundation of our reality, creating a self-fulfilling prophecy that reinforces the very assumptions we hold.

Understanding the power of beliefs is essential if we are to take control of our lives and create the reality we desire. By examining what we truly believe, we can begin to identify the beliefs that serve us and those that limit us. This process of introspection and transformation is key to unlocking our potential and living a life of purpose and fulfilment.

What Are Limiting Beliefs?

Limiting beliefs are the assumptions or convictions that we hold about ourselves, others, or the world that restrict our potential and hinder our growth. These beliefs are often negative and self-defeating, convincing us that we are not capable, worthy, or deserving of achieving our goals and desires. They create mental and emotional barriers that prevent us from pursuing our dreams, taking risks, or embracing new opportunities.

Some common examples of limiting beliefs include:

- **"I'm not good enough."**

- **"I don't deserve success."**

- **"People can't be trusted."**

- **"I'm too old/young to start something new."**

- **"Money is the root of all evil."**

- **"I'm not smart enough to succeed."**

- **"I'll never find true love."**

These beliefs often operate on a subconscious level, influencing our behavior in ways we may not even be aware of. They can stem from past experiences, societal conditioning, or the opinions of others, and they tend to be deeply ingrained in our psyche. As a result, limiting beliefs can be difficult to recognize and even harder to change.

How Limiting Beliefs Are Programmed in Childhood

Many of our limiting beliefs are formed during childhood, a period when we are highly impressionable and dependent on others for our understanding of the world. As children, we absorb the beliefs and attitudes of our parents, caregivers, teachers, and peers, often without questioning their validity. These early experiences and messages become the foundation of our belief system, shaping our self-image and worldview.

For example, if a child is repeatedly told that they are not smart enough or that they will never amount to anything, they may internalize these messages as truth. Over time, this belief becomes a part of their identity, influencing their actions and decisions well into adulthood. Similarly, if a child grows up in an environment where money is scarce and associated with stress or conflict, they may develop the belief that money is inherently bad or difficult to obtain.

These limiting beliefs are not always the result of direct messages. They can also arise from the way we interpret our experiences. A child who is bullied at school may come to believe that they are unlikable or that people are inherently cruel. A child who witnesses their parents struggling with their relationship may develop a belief that love is painful or that relationships are doomed to fail.

Because these beliefs are formed at such a young age, they often go unchallenged, becoming a default mode of thinking that influences our behavior in adulthood. Even when these beliefs no longer serve us, we may cling to them out of habit or because they provide a sense of familiarity and security.

The Impact of Limiting Beliefs

The impact of limiting beliefs on our lives can be profound. They shape our self-concept, determining what we believe is possible for us to achieve. When we hold limiting beliefs, we tend to play small, avoid risks, and settle for less than we deserve. These beliefs can lead to self-sabotage, procrastination, and a lack of motivation, preventing us from reaching our full potential.

For example, if you believe that you are not good enough, you may shy away from opportunities that could lead to growth or success. You might avoid applying for a job you want, starting a business, or pursuing a passion because you assume that you will fail or be rejected. Even if you do take action, this belief may cause you to doubt yourself at every step, undermining your efforts and ultimately leading to the very failure you feared.

Limiting beliefs can also affect our relationships, health, and overall well-being. If you believe that you are unworthy of love, you may attract partners who treat you poorly or stay in unhealthy relationships out of fear that you won't find anything better. If you believe that you are destined to be unhealthy, you may neglect your physical health or engage in self-destructive behaviors. These beliefs create a cycle of negativity that perpetuates itself, making it difficult to break free and create a better life.

How to Overcome Limiting Beliefs

Overcoming limiting beliefs is a process of self-discovery, awareness, and intentional change. It requires you to examine your beliefs, challenge their validity, and replace them with empowering beliefs that support your growth and success. Here are some steps to help you overcome your limiting beliefs:

1. Identify Your Limiting Beliefs

The first step in overcoming limiting beliefs is to identify them. This requires you to become aware of the thoughts and assumptions that guide your behavior and decision-making. Pay attention to the recurring patterns in your life, particularly in areas where you feel stuck or unfulfilled. Ask yourself the following questions:

- **What are the beliefs I hold about myself, others, and the world?**

- **What assumptions do I make about what is possible for me?**

- **Where do I feel limited or held back in my life?**

- **What fears or doubts consistently arise when I think about pursuing my goals?**

You can also identify limiting beliefs by examining the language you use. Notice if you frequently say things like "I can't," "I'm not," or "It's impossible." These phrases often point to underlying beliefs that are limiting your potential.

Journaling can be a helpful tool in this process. Write down your thoughts and feelings about different areas of your life—career, relationships, health, finances—and look for patterns or recurring themes. Be honest with yourself, and don't be afraid to dig deep. The more you uncover, the more empowered you will be to change.

2. Challenge the Validity of Your Beliefs

Once you have identified your limiting beliefs, the next step is to challenge their validity. Remember, beliefs are not facts—they are merely perceptions or interpretations of reality that can be changed. Ask yourself the following questions:

- **Is this belief objectively true?**

- **What evidence do I have to support this belief?**

- **Is there evidence that contradicts this belief?**

- **Where did this belief come from? Is it really mine, or did I inherit it from someone else?**

- **How has this belief served me in the past? How is it limiting me now?**

- **What would my life look like if I didn't hold this belief?**

By questioning the validity of your beliefs, you begin to weaken their hold on you. You may realize that many of your beliefs are based on past experiences that are no longer relevant or on the opinions of others that do not reflect your true self. This awareness creates the space for new, more empowering beliefs to emerge.

3. Replace Limiting Beliefs with Empowering Beliefs

After challenging your limiting beliefs, the next step is to replace them with empowering beliefs that support your growth and success. Empowering beliefs are positive, constructive thoughts that reflect your true potential and capabilities. They help you to see possibilities instead of limitations, to take action instead of procrastinating, and to pursue your goals with confidence and determination.

To create empowering beliefs, consider the following:

- **Reframe Negative Beliefs:** Turn your limiting beliefs into positive affirmations. For example, if your limiting belief is "I'm not good enough," reframe it as "I am capable and deserving of success." If your belief is "I can't trust people," reframe it as "I attract trustworthy and supportive people into my life."

- **Visualize Your Success:** Visualization is a powerful tool for reinforcing new beliefs. Spend time each day imagining yourself living out your new beliefs. See yourself achieving your goals, experiencing joy and fulfilment, and overcoming challenges with ease. The more vividly you can visualize your success, the more real it will become in your mind.

- **Practice Affirmations:** Affirmations are positive statements that you repeat to yourself to reinforce your new beliefs. Write down your empowering beliefs as affirmations and repeat them daily, especially in moments of doubt or fear. For example, you might say, "I am worthy of love and respect," "I have the skills and abilities to achieve my dreams," or "I create my reality with positive thoughts and actions." (We will delve deeper into these in the next chapter).

- **Take Action:** Empowering beliefs are strengthened by action. Start taking steps toward your goals, even if they are small. Each action you take reinforces the belief that you are capable and deserving of success. Celebrate your progress and use it as evidence that your new beliefs are true.

4. Surround Yourself with Positive Influences

The people and environments you surround yourself with can have a significant impact on your beliefs. If you are constantly around negative, critical, or limiting influences, it will be difficult to maintain your new, empowering beliefs. If you surround yourself with positive, supportive, and growth-oriented people, your new beliefs will be reinforced and strengthened.

Seek out relationships and communities that uplift and inspire you. Spend time with people who believe in you and encourage you to pursue your dreams. Engage in activities that align with your new beliefs, such as reading motivational books, attending personal development workshops, or participating in supportive groups or online communities.

Remember, you have the power to choose your influences. Be intentional about the people and environments you allow into your life, and protect your energy by distancing yourself from those that do not support your growth.

5. Practice Self-Compassion

Overcoming limiting beliefs is not always a linear process. There may be times when you slip back into old patterns of thinking or feel discouraged by setbacks. During these moments, it is important to practice self-compassion and be gentle with yourself.

Recognize that changing deeply ingrained beliefs takes time and effort. Celebrate your progress, no matter how small, and remind yourself that you are on a journey of growth and self-discovery. When you encounter challenges or setbacks, use them as opportunities to learn and grow, rather than as evidence that your new beliefs are not valid.

Self-compassion also means acknowledging your worth and treating yourself with kindness and respect. Speak to yourself as you would to a dear friend—encouraging, supportive, and understanding. The more you cultivate a compassionate relationship with yourself, the more resilient you will be in the face of challenges.

The Transformative Power of Belief

Beliefs are powerful creators of our reality. They shape our thoughts, emotions, and actions, influencing the life we experience. By identifying and overcoming limiting beliefs, you can reclaim your power and create a life that is aligned with your true potential and desires.

As you embark on this journey of transformation, remember that you are the author of your own story. You have the power to choose what you believe, and in doing so, you have the power to create the life you want. By replacing limiting beliefs with empowering ones, you open the door to new possibilities, opportunities, and experiences. You become the conscious creator of your reality, living a life of purpose, fulfilment, and joy.

Embrace the process of self-discovery and growth, and trust that with each step, you are moving closer to the life you desire. The power of belief is within you—use it wisely and intentionally, and watch as your life transforms before your eyes.

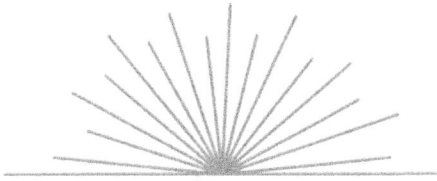

Chapter 14

The Transformative Power of Positive Affirmations: Rewriting Your Story and Changing Your Life

The Science Behind Positive Affirmations

Positive affirmations are more than just feel-good statements—they are powerful tools that can help you reshape your beliefs, rewire your brain, and ultimately transform your life. At their core, affirmations are statements or declarations that you repeat to yourself to reinforce positive thinking and beliefs. When practiced consistently, affirmations can help you challenge and overcome self-sabotaging and limiting beliefs, paving the way for personal growth, increased self-confidence, and the achievement of your goals.

The power of affirmations lies in their ability to influence your subconscious mind. Our subconscious is responsible for processing the vast majority of our thoughts, beliefs, and behaviors. It operates based on the information it has been fed over time, which includes the beliefs and assumptions we've internalized from our past experiences, upbringing, and societal influences. By using affirmations, you can begin to replace old, limiting beliefs with new, empowering ones, effectively reprogramming your subconscious mind to support your desires and aspirations.

Research in the field of neuroscience has shown that the brain is incredibly adaptable, a quality known as neuroplasticity. This means that our thoughts and behaviors can actually change the structure and function of our brain. When you repeat positive affirmations, you are creating new neural pathways that align with your desired beliefs and outcomes. Over time, these pathways become stronger, making it easier for you to adopt new, positive ways of thinking and acting.

Why Affirmations Work

Affirmations work because they engage several psychological and neurological processes simultaneously. Here's how they can help you change your life:

1. Cognitive Restructuring

Affirmations help to restructure your thought patterns by challenging and replacing negative or limiting beliefs with positive ones. This process, known as cognitive restructuring, involves identifying negative self-talk and consciously choosing to replace it with positive, empowering statements. For example, if you catch yourself thinking, "I'm not good enough," you can use the affirmation, "I am capable and deserving of success," to counteract that negative thought.

2. Self-Perception Theory

Self-perception theory suggests that we form our self-identity by observing our own behavior and the affirmations we make about ourselves. When you consistently use positive affirmations, you begin to see yourself in a new light, which can lead to changes in your behavior and actions. Over time, this can help you build a stronger sense of self-worth and confidence.

3. Visualization and Emotional Engagement

Affirmations are most effective when they are paired with visualization and emotional engagement. When you repeat an affirmation, take a moment to visualize yourself experiencing the outcome you desire. Imagine the feelings of joy, pride, and fulfilment that come with achieving your goals. This emotional engagement helps to anchor the affirmation in your subconscious, making it more likely that you will believe and act on it.

4. Breaking Negative Feedback Loops

Limiting beliefs often create negative feedback loops, where negative thoughts lead to negative behaviors, which in turn reinforce the original negative beliefs. For example, if you believe that you are not good at public speaking, you might avoid opportunities to speak in public, which reinforces your belief that you are not capable. Affirmations help to break these loops by introducing positive thoughts that lead to positive behaviors, thereby creating new, positive feedback loops.

Creating Effective Affirmations

Not all affirmations are created equal. For an affirmation to be effective, it needs to be specific, positive, and emotionally resonant. Here are some guidelines for creating powerful affirmations that can help you overcome your limiting beliefs and change your life:

1. Keep It Positive

Affirmations should always be framed in a positive light. Instead of focusing on what you want to avoid or eliminate, focus on what you want to attract or achieve. For example, instead of saying, "I don't want to be afraid of failure," say, "I embrace challenges and grow from every experience."

2. Use the Present Tense

Affirmations should be stated in the present tense, as if they are already true. This helps to create a sense of immediacy and reality in your mind. For example, say, "I am confident and successful," rather than "I will be confident and successful."

3. Be Specific

The more specific your affirmation, the more powerful it will be. Instead of using vague statements like "I am happy," try to be more detailed, such as "I am filled with joy and gratitude every day." This specificity helps your mind to visualize the desired outcome more clearly.

4. Make It Personal

Your affirmations should be deeply personal and meaningful to you. They should reflect your true desires and values, not what others expect or want from you. This personal connection makes the affirmation more emotionally resonant and effective.

5. Focus on the Feeling

Effective affirmations tap into the emotions associated with your desired outcome. Include words that evoke strong positive feelings, such as "joy," "love," "gratitude," or "confidence." For example, "I am surrounded by love and support" is more emotionally powerful than simply saying, "I am loved."

6. Keep It Simple

While it's important to be specific, it's also important to keep your affirmations simple and concise. A short, clear statement is easier to remember and repeat throughout the day. For example, "I am worthy of success" is a powerful and straightforward affirmation that can be easily integrated into your daily routine.

Using Affirmations to Overcome Limiting Beliefs

Now that you know how to create effective affirmations, it's time to put them to work to overcome your limiting beliefs that you discovered in the previous chapter. Here's a step-by-step process to help you use affirmations to transform your mindset and your life:

1. Identify Your Limiting Beliefs

Using your list of limiting beliefs, take some time to reflect on the areas of your life where you feel stuck, unfulfilled, or unhappy so that you can begin to address them. This list might not be written within the timeframe of reading this book- they might come to your attention as you go about your normal routines at work, with friends or when you are faced with a difficult situation.

2. Create Empowering Affirmations

Once you have identified and understand your limiting beliefs, create positive affirmations that directly counteract these beliefs. For each limiting belief, write an empowering affirmation that reflects the opposite of that belief. For example, if your limiting belief is "I'm not good enough," your affirmation might be "I am capable and worthy of achieving my dreams."

3. Repeat Your Affirmations Daily

Consistency is key when it comes to affirmations. Make a habit of repeating your affirmations every day, preferably multiple times throughout the day. You can say them out loud, write them down, or even think them silently in your mind. The more you repeat your affirmations, the more they will begin to influence your subconscious mind and replace your limiting beliefs.

4. Pair Affirmations with Visualization

To enhance the effectiveness of your affirmations, pair them with visualization. As you repeat your affirmations, close your eyes and imagine yourself living out the reality described by the affirmation. Picture yourself achieving your goals, feeling confident and successful, and experiencing the positive emotions associated with your desired outcome. Visualization helps to make your affirmations feel more real and attainable.

5. Incorporate Affirmations into Your Daily Routine

To make affirmations a natural part of your life, incorporate them into your daily routine. You can repeat your affirmations during your morning routine, while exercising, during meditation, or before going to bed. You might also consider placing written affirmations in visible places, such as on your mirror, refrigerator, or workspace, as constant reminders of your new beliefs.

6. Be Patient and Persistent

Changing deeply ingrained beliefs takes time and effort, so be patient with yourself as you work with affirmations. You may not see immediate results, but with persistence and consistency, you will begin to notice shifts in your thinking, behavior, and overall life experience. Remember, affirmations are a tool for long-term transformation, and their power lies in their cumulative effect over time.

Examples of Positive Affirmations

To help you get started, here are some examples of positive affirmations that you can use or adapt to suit your own needs and goals:

1. Self-Worth and Confidence

- "I am worthy of love, respect, and success."

- "I believe in my abilities and trust myself to succeed."

- "I am confident, capable, and strong."

2. Abundance and Prosperity

- "I attract abundance and prosperity into my life."

- "I am open to receiving all the wealth life offers me."

- "I deserve financial success and the freedom it brings."

3. Health and Well-Being

- "I am healthy, vibrant, and full of energy."

- "My body is strong, my mind is clear, and my heart is at peace."

- "I nurture my body with love and care."

4. Relationships and Love

- "I am surrounded by love and support."

- "I attract positive, healthy relationships into my life."

- "I am deserving of deep, meaningful connections."

5. Personal Growth and Success

- "I am constantly growing, evolving, and becoming my best self."

- "I am committed to achieving my goals and manifesting my dreams."

- "I embrace challenges as opportunities for growth and learning."

Transforming Your Life with Affirmations

Positive affirmations are a simple yet profoundly effective tool for changing your life. By consciously choosing to focus on empowering thoughts and beliefs, you can begin to rewrite your story and create the life you truly desire. Remember, the key to success with affirmations is consistency, emotional engagement, and a deep belief in the possibility of change.

As you integrate affirmations into your daily life, you will begin to notice shifts in your mindset, behavior, and circumstances. Your limiting beliefs will gradually lose their power, making way for new, positive beliefs that support your growth and success. With time, you will become the person you've always wanted to be—confident, empowered, and living a life of purpose and fulfilment.

So, take the first step today. Start by identifying one limiting belief that has been holding you back and create a positive affirmation to counteract it. Repeat this affirmation daily, visualize your success, and watch as your life begins to transform. The power to change your life is within you—use it wisely and with intention, and the results will be nothing short of extraordinary.

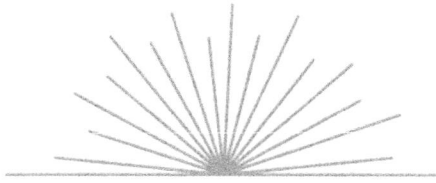

Chapter 15

The Core Practice of Neville Goddard's Law of Assumption

Introduction

Neville Goddard was a 20th-century manifestation teacher and was renowned for his teachings on the Law of Assumption, a powerful concept rooted in the belief that consciousness shapes reality. This book offers an in-depth exploration and modern interpretation of Neville Goddard's Law of Assumption principles, bridging timeless wisdom with contemporary insights. By delving into Goddard's foundational idea that our beliefs and assumptions shape our reality, and through the steps outlined in this book, you will gain practical tools and actionable strategies to apply these principles in today's world. Whether you're familiar with Goddard's teachings or new to the concept, this book serves as a comprehensive guide to understanding and harnessing the power of your mind to manifest the life you desire. However, it is important to understand the origins of these principles and grasp Neville's core concepts. Below, I have provided a brief overview of his teachings to give you a foundational understanding and help you grasp, embed and deepen the core concepts that have been explored in this book.

Central to Goddard's philosophy is the idea that one's assumptions, rather than external circumstances, dictate the experiences and outcomes in life. The Law of Assumption, as Goddard teaches it, provides a framework for individuals to consciously create the life they desire by assuming the feeling of their wish fulfilled.

This chapter delves into the main practice of the Law of Assumption, exploring its foundational principles, techniques, and the profound impact it can have on one's life. We will uncover how to effectively apply this practice, common challenges, and the transformative power it holds when properly understood and implemented.

The Foundation of the Law of Assumption

At the heart of the Law of Assumption is the concept that our external reality is a direct reflection of our internal state—specifically, our beliefs and assumptions. Goddard posited that the world around us is not something that happens to us but something that happens through us. In his view, reality is malleable, shaped by the assumptions we hold about ourselves and our world.

Goddard emphasized the importance of assuming the feeling of the wish fulfilled—a practice where one imagines and feels as though their desire has already been realized. This assumption, when sustained, alters the state of consciousness, which in turn influences the subconscious mind to bring about the desired outcome. Goddard believed that by aligning one's thoughts and feelings with the desired reality, one could effectively bring it into existence.

The Central Practice: Feeling Is the Secret

The core practice of the Law of Assumption revolves around the principle encapsulated in Goddard's statement, "Feeling is the secret." This phrase underscores the importance of not just thinking about one's desires but deeply feeling the emotions associated with having already achieved them.

To truly embody the practice of the Law of Assumption, one must cultivate a deep emotional connection to their desired outcome. This process involves a few key steps:

1. Clarify Your Desire: The first step is to clearly identify what it is you truly want. This could be a specific goal, a change in circumstances, or a personal transformation. The more specific and vivid the desire, the easier it is to focus on it in the subsequent steps.

2. Create a Mental Image: Once the desire is clear, the next step is to create a detailed mental image of it. This involves visualizing the scenario in which your desire has already been fulfilled. For example, if your desire is to be in a loving relationship, imagine a scene that implies you are already in that relationship—perhaps a conversation with your partner or a shared moment of joy.

3. Feel the Emotions: This step is crucial. As you visualize your desire, focus on the emotions you would feel if your desire were already a reality. How would you feel waking up every day knowing your desire has been fulfilled? What emotions would accompany this new reality? The goal is to immerse yourself fully in these feelings, allowing them to permeate your entire being.

4. Saturate Your Consciousness: After establishing the feeling of the wish fulfilled, the next step is to sustain it. This means regularly revisiting your mental image and the associated emotions, especially during quiet moments like before sleep or during meditation. The more frequently and vividly you can feel these emotions, the more deeply they will impress upon your subconscious mind.

5. Live From the End: Living from the end means carrying the assumption that your desire has already been realized in your day-to-day life. This doesn't necessarily mean pretending or deluding

113

yourself; rather, it involves holding a quiet, confident belief that your desire is already yours. This belief should influence your actions, thoughts, and decisions, aligning them with the reality of your fulfilled desire.

Techniques to Amplify the Practice

Neville Goddard introduced several techniques to help individuals more effectively engage with the Law of Assumption. These techniques are designed to deepen the emotional experience and reinforce the feeling of the wish fulfilled.

1. The Imaginal Scene: Goddard often spoke of creating an "imaginal scene" that implies the fulfilment of your desire. This scene should be short, vivid, and looped repeatedly in your mind until it feels natural and real. For instance, if your desire is to land a dream job, you might imagine a scene where you are shaking hands with your new boss, receiving congratulations, or even discussing your first successful project.

The key is to make this scene as real as possible in your mind, engaging all your senses—what you see, hear, feel, and even smell. By doing this, you saturate your consciousness with the feeling of the wish fulfilled.

2. The State Akin to Sleep (SATS): Goddard emphasized the importance of practicing the Law of Assumption in a state akin to sleep—a drowsy, relaxed state of consciousness that occurs just before falling asleep or upon waking. In this state, the mind is highly receptive to suggestions and images.

During SATS, you should focus on your desired outcome, imagining it as vividly as possible while feeling the emotions associated with it. Because the subconscious is most impressionable in this state, it is an ideal time to impress your desire upon it.

3. Inner Conversations: Another powerful technique involves altering your inner conversations. These are the dialogues you have with

yourself throughout the day. According to Goddard, these internal dialogues shape your reality as much as your external actions.

To practice this technique, become aware of your inner conversations and consciously redirect them to align with the fulfilment of your desire. If you catch yourself thinking negatively or doubting your desire, gently but firmly replace those thoughts with positive affirmations that reinforce the belief that your desire is already realized.

4. Revision: The technique of revision involves reimagining past events in a way that aligns with your desired outcome. Goddard taught that by revising past experiences—especially those that were negative or limiting—you can change the emotional impact they have on you and, consequently, alter your present and future reality.

To practice revision, select a memory that did not go the way you wanted. Then, in your mind, replay the event, but this time imagine it unfolding in a way that fulfils your desire. Feel the emotions of this revised version of events as though they truly happened, and allow this new memory to replace the old one in your consciousness.

Overcoming Challenges

While the Law of Assumption is a powerful tool for manifestation, it is not without its challenges. Many people struggle with doubts, negative thoughts, and deeply ingrained beliefs that contradict their desires. These challenges can make it difficult to fully embrace the feeling of the wish fulfilled.

1. Doubt and Limiting Beliefs: One of the most common obstacles is doubt. Doubts often arise when there is a gap between one's current reality and the desired outcome. These doubts can be fueled by limiting beliefs—deep-seated convictions that contradict the desired assumption. For instance, if someone desires financial abundance but holds a belief that money is hard to come by, this belief can undermine the assumption of wealth.

To overcome doubt and limiting beliefs, remember, repetition is key; the more you affirm your desired reality, the more you weaken the hold of limiting beliefs.

2.   Persistence: Another challenge is maintaining persistence in the face of external circumstances that appear contrary to your desired outcome. Goddard emphasized the importance of persistence, noting that the Law of Assumption requires a sustained focus on the desired state.

Persistence means continually returning to the feeling of the wish fulfilled, even when circumstances seem unchanged. It involves a deep trust in the process and a willingness to keep going, knowing that reality will eventually conform to the assumption.

3.   Impatience: Many people struggle with impatience, expecting immediate results from their practice of the Law of Assumption. When results don't materialize as quickly as desired, it can lead to frustration and a sense of failure.

To counteract impatience, it's important to remember that the Law of Assumption is not about instant gratification but about aligning with a higher state of consciousness. Results will manifest in their own time, according to the natural unfolding of events. Trust in the process and remain focused on the feeling of the wish fulfilled, knowing that it will come to pass.

The Power of Faith and Imagination

Faith and imagination are the twin pillars that support the practice of the Law of Assumption. Neville Goddard emphasized that imagination is the creative force of the universe, and faith is the substance that gives form to the imagined reality.

1.   Imagination as Reality: Goddard believed that imagination is not just a mental exercise but the very fabric of reality. What you imagine with feeling and conviction becomes real in the world. Therefore, cultivating a vivid and detailed imagination is crucial for effectively practicing the Law of Assumption.

Engage your imagination regularly, not just during formal practice sessions but throughout your day. Use your imagination to see the world as you wish it to be, rather than as it currently appears. Over time, this imaginative exercise will reshape your perception and, by extension, your reality.

2. Faith as the Bridge: Faith, in the context of the Law of Assumption, is the belief in things unseen—the conviction that your desired reality exists even if you cannot yet perceive it with your physical senses. Faith acts as a bridge between the imagined world and the physical world.

Cultivating faith involves trusting in the power of your assumptions and in the process of manifestation. It requires letting go of the need to control how and when your desires will manifest, and instead focusing on the end result with unwavering confidence.

Transformative Impact of the Law of Assumption

When practiced consistently and with conviction, the Law of Assumption can lead to profound transformations in every area of life—relationships, health, career, finances, and personal growth.

1. Relationships: By assuming the feeling of being loved, valued, and respected, individuals can attract and nurture healthy, fulfilling relationships. This practice can also heal existing relationships by shifting the focus from past hurts to the desired state of harmony and love.

2. Health: The Law of Assumption can be applied to health by assuming the feeling of vibrant well-being. By focusing on the emotions associated with perfect health—such as energy, vitality, and ease—individuals can influence their physical state and promote healing.

3. Career and Finances: In the realm of career and finances, the Law of Assumption can be a powerful tool for overcoming obstacles and achieving success. By assuming the feeling of financial abundance and career satisfaction, individuals can open doors to new opportunities and attract prosperity.

4. Personal Growth: The Law of Assumption is also a powerful tool for personal growth. By assuming the feeling of being confident, wise, and capable, individuals can overcome self-doubt and step into their full potential.

Real-Life Examples

Numerous real-life examples illustrate the transformative power of the Law of Assumption. From ordinary individuals to successful entrepreneurs, many have shared stories of how they used this practice to achieve remarkable results.

1. Financial Success: One man, struggling with financial difficulties, began practicing the Law of Assumption by imagining himself as financially secure. He visualized paying his bills with ease and feeling abundant. Over time, opportunities for increased income appeared, and his financial situation improved dramatically.

2. Healing and Recovery: A woman diagnosed with a serious illness used the Law of Assumption to support her healing journey. She imagined herself healthy, vibrant, and full of energy. Along with medical treatment, her positive assumptions played a crucial role in her recovery.

3. Career Advancement: Another individual, feeling stuck in a dead-end job, applied the Law of Assumption by imagining herself in her dream position. She visualized the joy and satisfaction of working in a role she loved. Within months, she was offered a new job that perfectly matched her imagined scenario.

Conclusion: Mastering the Law of Assumption

The Law of Assumption is a profound practice that empowers individuals to take control of their reality by aligning their thoughts, feelings, and beliefs with their desired outcomes. It is a practice that requires dedication, persistence, and faith, but the rewards are immense.

By mastering the core principles of the Law of Assumption—clarifying desires, cultivating the feeling of the wish fulfilled, and sustaining this feeling through imagination and faith—anyone can transform their life. Whether the goal is to improve relationships, achieve financial success, or promote personal growth, the Law of Assumption offers a path to realizing one's fullest potential.

This book has outlines how to heal and change the way you look at yourself and the world around you as Neville Goddard taught, "Change your conception of yourself and you will automatically change the world in which you live." This statement encapsulates the power and simplicity of the Law of Assumption. It is not the external world that needs to change but the internal assumptions that shape our perception of it. By changing these assumptions, we change our world.

This book and the practice of the Law of Assumption are more than a technique; it is a way of life—a journey of self-discovery and self-mastery that leads to a deeper understanding of the creative power within each of us. As you embark on this journey, remember that the power to shape your reality lies not in the circumstances around you but within your own consciousness.

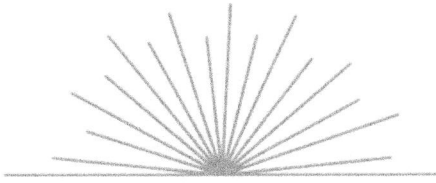

Chapter 16

Living in the End—Becoming What You Desire by Embracing the Present Moment

In the journey of self-transformation, one of the most powerful concepts is living as though you already are what you wish to be, with all your desires already fulfilled. This principle, popularized by mystics like Neville Goddard, teaches us that the key to manifesting our dreams lies in embodying the state of our fulfilled desires in the present moment. It's about aligning your thoughts, emotions, and actions with the reality you wish to create, even if it feels like you're pretending or being delusional. The truth is, what you focus on, you become. By living "in the end" and assuming the feeling of your wish fulfilled, you begin to attract the circumstances, opportunities, and experiences that match that state.

The Power of Living as If

The essence of Neville Goddard's teachings is that "imagination creates reality." By imagining the end result of what you desire and living from that state as if it's already true, you align yourself with the reality you want to manifest. This isn't just daydreaming; it's about fully immersing yourself in the feeling and experience of your desired state right now, in this moment. Imagine you already are the person you want to become. If you desire more confidence, wealth, love, or success, ask yourself: How would I feel, think, and act if I already had it? How would I carry myself? What would my mindset be like? By consistently embodying those feelings and behaviors in the present moment, you begin to shift your reality.

We Get What We Are, Not What We Want

A profound aspect of manifesting is understanding that we attract not what we simply wish for, but what we are. Our dominant state of being—the energy we consistently radiate—determines what we attract into our lives. This is why it's essential to focus on embodying the qualities you desire rather than just longing for them. If you want to attract love, become love. If you desire abundance, adopt the mindset and energy of abundance. If you seek peace, cultivate inner peace now, regardless of external circumstances. The external world is a reflection of your internal state, so the more you embody what you desire, the more you naturally attract it. This shift from wanting to being is where true transformation occurs. Wanting something implies lack, whereas being suggests fulfilment. By living from the state of already being fulfilled, you bypass the energy of lack and align with the vibration of having. You stop chasing and start allowing, which is when things start to flow naturally into your life.

The Present Moment: The Gateway to Your Desired Reality

The present moment is where all transformation takes place. It's easy to get lost in either dwelling on the past or worrying about the future, but the present is the only moment where you can consciously choose to embody the state of your desired reality. The more you anchor yourself in the present, the more control you have over your internal state and, ultimately, your life's trajectory. Neville Goddard emphasized that imagining your desired reality as something distant or in the future keeps it there—in the future. Instead, by bringing that reality into the now and fully feeling its presence as if it's already here, you collapse the timeline and draw it into your experience. You are training your subconscious mind to accept this new state as your default reality, and in time, your external world will mirror that belief. Use the present moment to focus on the feeling of your wish fulfilled. What does it feel like to be the person you want to be, to have the life you desire? Sink into that feeling, let it permeate your being, and return to it often. Make it a habit to visit your desired state throughout the day, whether through visualization, affirmations, or simply holding onto that feeling of fulfilment. The more you practice this, the more natural it becomes, and the faster your external reality shifts to match it.

Embodying Your Future Self Today

To truly live as if your desires are already fulfilled, start making decisions and taking actions from the mindset of your future self. If you already were the confident, successful, or loving person you aspire to be, what choices would you make? How would you spend your time? Who would you associate with? Begin aligning your current life with these choices, no matter how small the steps might be. This approach doesn't mean ignoring your current responsibilities or pretending that challenges don't exist. It's about aligning your thoughts and actions with the person you want to become. Over time, these small, consistent shifts create momentum and bring you closer to your desired reality.

Letting Go and Trusting the Process

While living in the end and embodying your desires is key, it's equally important to let go of attachment to how and when your desires will manifest. Trust that once you've planted the seed in your imagination and consistently nurtured it through your thoughts and feelings, the universe will orchestrate the perfect circumstances for its realization. Your job is to live in the state of already having it, to act as if it's already done, and to let go of the need to control every detail. Trust that your desires are on their way, and in the meantime, continue to embody the state of your wish fulfilled. Keep aligning with the energy of what you want, knowing that it's not just about getting something in the future, but about transforming who you are in the present.

Becoming What You Focus On

In the end, we become what we focus on the most. By living as if your desires are already fulfilled and embodying the state of your ideal self in the present moment, you align with the reality you wish to create. The world reflects back to us what we are, not just what we want. So become the energy you wish to experience, even if it feels like you're imagining it at first. As you continue to practice living in the end, your imagination will solidify into reality. Remember, the present moment holds the power to reshape your life. It's in the now that you choose who you are and what you attract. Step into the reality you desire, feel it fully, and trust that as you do, the world will mirror back to you everything you've become. By living as though your dreams are already yours, you turn them into your reality—one moment, one thought, and one feeling at a time.

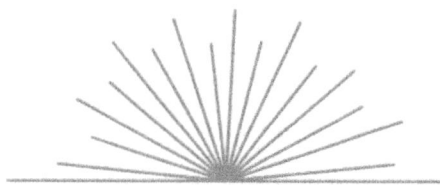

Printed in Dunstable, United Kingdom

76155797R00070